P9-DHI-178

DORLING KINDERSLEY DK EYEWITNESS BOOKS

SPY

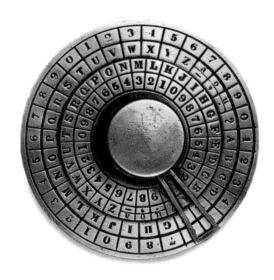

Night-vision
goggles

Handheld
transmitter

Laptop computer
trace showing
presence of bug
in a building

James Bond's
piton gun from
Goldeneye

Side view of
explosives pack for
stay-behind agents
in the event of World
War III occurring

Ultraviolet
lantern and
anti-bugging
seals

Prints made by SOE agent's rubber
soles used to disguise beach landings

Ox tongue tin for
muggling maps and
mpasses, World War I

German invisible ink
and sponge

DK EYEWITNESS BOOKS

SPY

Written by
Richard Platt
Photographed by
Geoff Dann and Steve Gorton

SOE rubber soles
worn on boots to
disguise landings on
beaches and in deserts

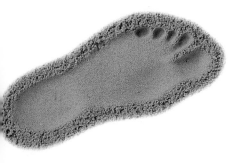

ather boot heel
h concealed
npartment,
rld
r II

Message hidden
in rubber boot
heel, World
War II

Dorling Kindersley

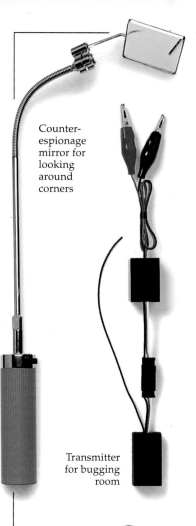

Counter-
espionage
mirror for
looking
around
corners

Transmitter
for bugging
room

Doll made in Fresnes
prison, France, by World
War II agent Odette Sansom

Dorling Kindersley
LONDON, NEW YORK, DELHI, JOHANNESBURG, MUNICH, PARIS and SYDNEY

For a full catalog, visit

Project editor Miranda Smith
Art editor Kati Poynor
Assistant editor Julie Ferris
Managing editor Gillian Denton
Managing art editor Julia Harris
Production Charlotte Trail
Picture research Sarah Moule

This Eyewitness ® Book has been conceived by
Dorling Kindersley Limited and Editions Gallimard

© 1996 Dorling Kindersley Limited
This edition © 2000 Dorling Kindersley Limited
First American edition, 1996

Published in the United States by
Dorling Kindersley Publishing, Inc.
375 Hudson Street,
New York, NY 10014
16 18 20 19 17

Dorling Kindersley books are available at special discounts for bulk purchases
for sales promotions or premiums. Special editions, including personalized
covers, excerpts of existing guides, and corporate imprints can be created in large
quantities for specific needs. For more information, contact Special Markets.

Library of Congress Cataloging-in-Publication Data
Platt, Richard.
Spy / written by Richard Platt.
p. cm. — (Eyewitness Books) Includes index.
Summary: Presents information about men and women spies
throughout history as well as about the tools and equipment they
used in espionage and intelligence service.
1. Espionage—History—Juvenile literature. 2. Intelligence
service—History—Juvenile literature. [1. Espionage—History.
2. Intelligence service—History.] I. Title. II.Series.
JF1525.16P583 2000   327.12—dc20   96–11003
ISBN 13: 978-0-7894-5852-0 (HB)
ISBN-13: 978-0-7894-6616-7 (ALB)

Color reproduction by Colourscan, Singapore
Printed in China by Toppan Printing Co. (Shenzhen) Ltd.

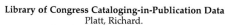

Silk map of
France used
by wartime
agent

Handheld
transmitter
or "bug"

Matchbox created for Special
Operations Executive agent

Contents

Capsule for
suicide pill,
World War II

Suicide pill,
World War II

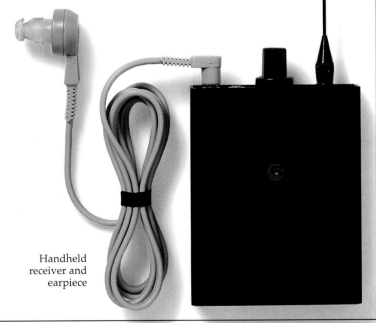

Handheld
receiver and
earpiece

What is a spy?

SPYING, WHICH IS ALSO called espionage, began thousands of years ago, with nations battling for land, wealth, or slaves. Spies sneaked into the camps of their enemies, counting the number of warriors or looking for plans of attack. If they were successful, they returned as heroes with the "intelligence," secrets, they had uncovered. Those who were caught faced execution. Throughout history governments and businesses have hidden their most important documents, very often marking them with special phrases such as "TOP SECRET" or "CONFIDENTIAL," and allowing only a few trusted people to see them. Spies are hired by other nations or businesses to find out this secret information. Spies still live dangerous lives today. Some work like burglars to collect intelligence. Others have access to secrets only because other people trust them. By betraying that trust, a spy can win or lose wars, and even change the course of history.

Rahab marked her windows with a red cord

Joshua watches as the walls of Jericho tumble down

Tapestry shows spies from both sides in the Battle of Hastings

BIBLE ESPIONAGE
A story in the Old Testament, the holy book of Judaism and Christianity, tells how spies helped defeat the walled city of Jericho. The leader of the attacking army, Joshua, sent two spies into the town at dusk. They went to the house of a prostitute, Rahab, and hid on the roof. Rahab lied to the Jericho authorities to protect the spies, and when Joshua's troops destroyed the city, they spared the lives of Rahab and her family, but killed everybody else.

EGYPTIAN SPY
Ankhesenamen, young queen of Egypt, wanted to remarry when her husband, Tutankhamen, died in 1324 B.C. She wrote to a neighboring king: "Send me one of your grown-up sons ... he shall be king over Egypt." Instead, the king sent his assistant as a spy to check the queen's story.

SPYING FOR THE MONGOLS
Spies helped Genghis Khan (1162–1227) to conquer most of Asia. Genghis came from Mongolia in central Asia, but he knew that people from Mongolia would soon arouse suspicion in distant lands. So Khan shrewdly recruited spies from among the target peoples, and these local spies were able to move around freely, collecting intelligence. Over longer distances, he used horsemen who could ride ten times faster than a marching army to carry his secret messages.

In the east, the Mongol empire reached the Pacific

ALEXANDER THE GREAT
The Macedonian king Alexander the Great (356–323 B.C.) used spies to find out about enemies' troop movements, and also to scout the best marching routes for his massive armies. Alexander's spies used a simple but effective technique to keep their messages secret. They wrote on narrow scrolls spiraling around a stick. Unwinding the scroll broke up the words of the message. But when wound around an identical stick, the text was easy to read.

The Bayeux Tapestry is actually embroidery on a linen strip 230 ft (70 m) long

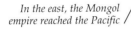

UNNOTICED IN THE CROWD
Some of the greatest spies of the past have been female: women could often go unnoticed where a man would arouse suspicion. In wartime, almost all young men joined the armed forces, and a man in civilian clothes was an unusual sight. In this photograph of Dutch spies at work during World War II (1939–45), one of the women takes a picture with a hidden camera.

Patterned bag hides camera lens

Fictional spy "007" was given a special "license to kill"

RECORDED FOR POSTERITY
The Bayeux Tapestry shows spies in the historic Battle of Hastings in England in 1066. The tapestry records how an army from northwest France, led by William of Normandy (1028–1087), conquered England in 1066. English spies reported sighting thousands of clean-shaven men with short hair. At that time in England, all men except priests wore mustaches and long hair, so the spies assumed that they had seen thousands of French priests. In fact, these "priests" were soldiers, who greatly outnumbered the English.

FICTIONAL SPIES
Glamorous spy James Bond, agent 007, is the hero of 13 novels by English author Ian Lancaster Fleming (1908–64). Fleming was himself a spy before he began his career as a writer. He used the people he met during that time as models for the characters in his books. The plots of the books and the Bond films leave out the routine side of the lives of real spies. However, some of Fleming's own exploits were as daring as those of the fictional agent 007.

Types of spy

SPIES COME FROM many different backgrounds and are recruited by an espionage agency for a variety of reasons. Many spies are attracted by money, but some are motivated by deeply held beliefs and are called "walk-in" spies because they require no persuasion. Others spy because they are being blackmailed, and still more because it makes them feel important. As "plants," spies penetrate (work their way into) a target organization, where they can collect intelligence. However, recruiting an "agent in place" is sometimes easier than penetration. These trusted insiders have access to secrets even before an agency recruits them – perhaps by using bribery or blackmail.

TROUBADOURS
These medieval minstrels went from castle to castle entertaining European nobles. Some spied by listening to royal gossip and repeating the news when they traveled to another country.

Walker tramped Vienna's streets while Soviet agents checked that he was not being followed

Building (indicated by red arrow on map) mentioned in Walker's typed instructions for a 1978 visit to Vienna

CARELESS TA...
Spies do not m...
themselves obvi...
by wearing unifor...
This wartime poster warned British citiz...
that they should not gossip about sons...
husbands in the armed forces because "Care...
talk costs lives." Bus passengers listening to...
conversation might be spies and could re...
details of troop movements to the ene...

WALK-IN WALKER
American John Walker worked for the U.S. Navy and sold intelligence to the Soviet Union for 17 years. To meet them for payment and training, his Soviet handlers usually instructed Walker to travel to Vienna, Austria.

INSIDER TRAPPED
French ambassador to Moscow Maurice Dejean unknowingly hired spies to work as his driver and maid. They used blackmail to try and turn him into an "agent in place." The plot failed, but Dejean's career was ruined.

The splendidly dressed Russian diplomats are "boyars" – members of noble Russian families

AMATEUR SPIES

nce Biblical times,
ders have kept
eir eyes and ears open
de when they traveled
road. These "amateur spies"
e returning home from the
nd of Canaan to report what
they have seen.

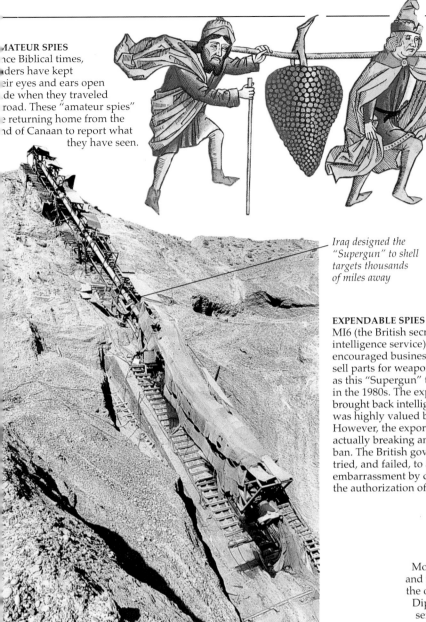

Iraq designed the
"Supergun" to shell
targets thousands
of miles away

EXPENDABLE SPIES

MI6 (the British secret
intelligence service)
encouraged businesses to
sell parts for weapons such
as this "Supergun" to Iraq
in the 1980s. The exporters
brought back intelligence that
was highly valued by MI6.
However, the exporters were
actually breaking an arms
ban. The British government
tried, and failed, to avoid
embarrassment by denying
the authorization of the sales.

MOLE IN THE CIA

Enemy agents who penetrate the security
services sometimes earn the nickname of
"mole," because they dig deep and work
invisibly. Chinese-American mole Larry
Wu Tai Chin worked for the CIA for
more than 35 years. From the beginning
he was a mole and was spying for China.

SPIES AT COURT

Most spies are "illegals" – if they are caught, they face prosecution
and punishment. Throughout history, traders and merchants, such as
the ones in this 16th-century woodcut, have been used as "illegals."
Diplomats, on the other hand, are often called "legals." These civil
servants represent their country in its embassies abroad, and they
have a license to spy. If they are caught, their diplomatic status
protects them from punishment under international law. In fact, very
few actually work as spies. More are intelligence officers – they use
their diplomatic jobs as a cover for recruiting and controlling spies.

ocession of diplomats and merchants at the
urt of the Austrian archduke Maximilian II

11

Secret tool kit

THE CENTRAL INTELLIGENCE AGENCY (CIA) nickname "sneakies" neatly describes the tools, gadgets, and weapons on which undercover agents often rely. With the aid of a sneaky, a spy can "bug" a conversation or photograph a meeting. Other devices make escape easier or hide the evidence of espionage from prying eyes. Fictional spy James Bond made sneakies famous. Before a dangerous mission, he visited the workshop of "Q," who built such gadgets. Autho[r] Ian Fleming based Q's character on the inventor Charles Fra[s] Smith (1904–92), who designed the equipment for the Britis[h] intelligence services in World War II. Other organizations ha[ve] equally ingenious spy workshops – for example, Stanley Lovell (1890–1976) equipped spies in the United States.

A spoof spy kit for the wartime spy

Pushing the two halves of the camera together advances the film by one frame and covers the lens

MINOX EC

1:5.6/15 mm

Lens is focused here

SUPER SMALL SNAPPER
The Minox camera is small enough to hide in a fist, but takes photographs of excellent quality. The Latvian manufacturers originally sold the Minox as a pocket-size camera, but the intelligence services quickly realized its potential and it became standard spy equipment. The camera's only real problem was the tiny size of its negatives, which needed to be enlarged 25 times to be read. At this small scale a speck of dust on the film could obscure a vital word.

Pen writes normally

HANDY HEEL
Concealed items must be well hidden to escape discovery, and shoes and boots can hide quite large weapons or tools. In World War II, spies sometimes concealed gold, for bribery, and knives in their insoles.

Thread is pulled to withdraw concealed item

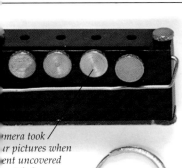

Exposures took minutes, so fixed objects such as buildings were the only practical subjects

Acoustic tube to microphone

...mera took ...ur pictures when ...ent uncovered ...e pinholes

...NHOLE CAMERA
...me of the tiniest spy ...meras use pinholes instead of a ...ns. KGB agents used this one in the ...80s. The camera takes pictures ...at are not blurred however ...ose or far away the ...bject. Although, ...thing is really ...arp either!

LISTENING PEN
The circuits of radio transmitters are now so small that spies can install bugs (small microphones) in the tiniest of objects. This pen is inconspicuous in a pocket, and would not attract attention in a desk drawer. However, it conceals a bug to eavesdrop on any nearby conversation. A tiny transmitter broadcasts the signal on UHF radio frequencies. The power of the signal is low, but strong enough for an accomplice sitting in a car almost 1,640 ft (500 m) away to pick up the conversation with a receiver and record it.

Body of pen conceals transmitter

A BRUSH WITH THE ENEMY
All spies risk capture, but the danger is perhaps even greater in wartime. So World War II spies hid all kinds of escape equipment in objects like this hairbrush. A compartment contains a saw to cut through prison bars, a map of enemy-occupied territory, and a compass.

Pulling bristles lifts compartment lid

Tube houses battery with enough power for up to six hours

Miniature saw blade

Compass
Compass needle

Devices hidden in hairbrush

EASY ACCESS
The safest way to enter a locked building is to bribe a low-paid employee to unlock the door. When this is not possible, spies may try to pick the lock with specially shaped tools like ...hese. In Britain, intelligence services employed a retired burglar to teach this vital skill to wartime agents.

By inserting one of the hooked blades into a lock and turning gently, the tool lifts levers that hold the bolt in place

Map printed on thin paper to fold up small

Base of brush is hollow

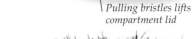

Specially shaped instruments are called picklocks

Range of picklocks enables agent to tackle locks of different sizes

Picks fold away into penknife-like handle

CHEATING AT CARDS
World War II spies concealed an escape map in a pack of playing cards. Tearing each card apart revealed a small area of the map. The numbers on each section allowed the spy to piece the whole map together like a jigsaw.

Seeing the invisibl

VISUAL SURVEILLANCE is part of the training of all agents. They learn to use their eyes and their cameras to collect intelligence or to gather information to blackmail their enemies. They use technology to make their vision keener. Magnifying lenses give a closer view of private scenes, while some night-vision equipment makes photography possible even in a candlelit bedroom. However, the clearest pictures do not guarantee the success of a surveillance mission. When spies secretly photographed a Western diplomat with his girlfriend, they were sure they could use the pictures for blackmail. They met the diplomat and threatened to send the pictures to his wife. His shameless response shocke them. "What wonderful shots!" he exclaimed. "Can you make me copies?

NOSY NEIGHBORS
The well-equipped spy does not need to stretch to get a better view.

Agent using a night-vision pen

CAUGHT IN THE ACT
To photograph subjects in near darkness, spies can use image-intensifier cameras. These use a tube similar to those fitted to night-vision equipment (opposite). The camera makes photography possible in extremely dim conditions; the glow of a cigarette provides ample light to photograph an agent copying documents or passing secrets to an accomplice. Image intensifiers cannot record color, so spies usually load their cameras with sensitive black-and-white film. In color (left), pictures have an eerie green glow.

A spy can swap a standard lens for a powerful telephoto

Replacing camera with an eyepiece turns the tube into a night vision telescope

Ordinary flashlight batteries in b provide pow

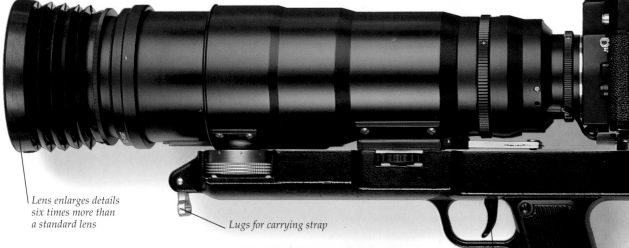

Lens enlarges details six times more than a standard lens

Lugs for carrying strap

"Trigger" operates shutter

The rifle grip he steady camera a keeps photograp sharp when it is impractical to use a tripod

An ordinary lens takes in the whole of the street market.

"Photo-sniper" camera picks out two particular figures from the crowd.

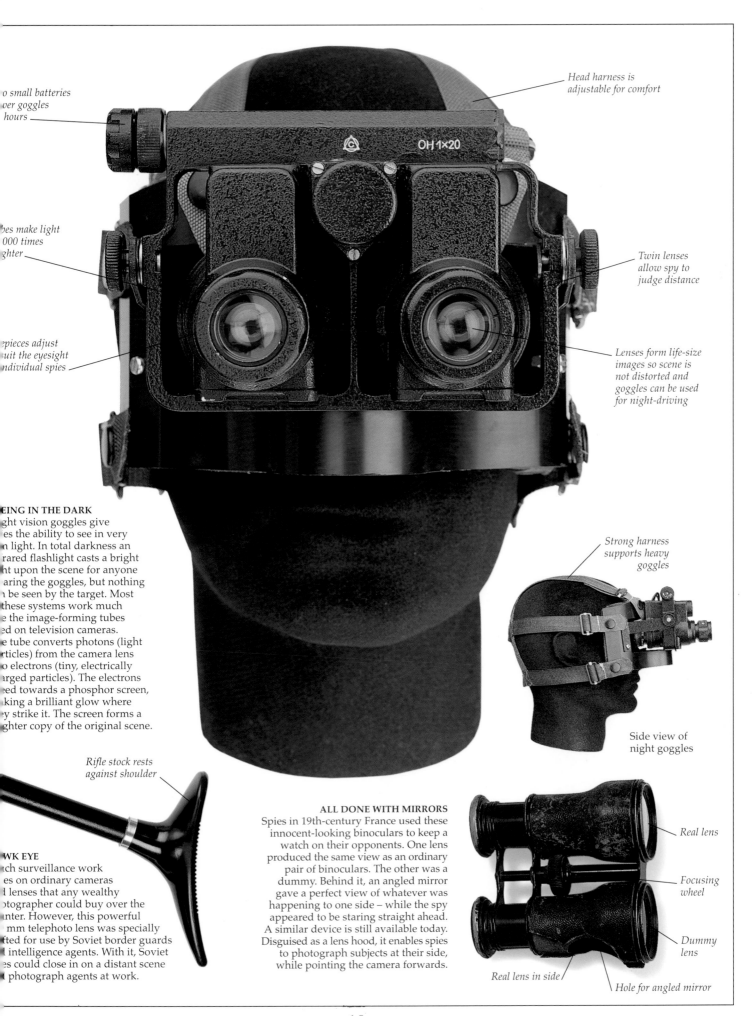

Head harness is
adjustable for comfort

OH 1×20

Twin lenses
allow spy to
judge distance

Lenses form life-size
images so scene is
not distorted and
goggles can be used
for night-driving

...o small batteries
...wer goggles
... hours

...es make light
...000 times
...ghter

...pieces adjust
...uit the eyesight
...ndividual spies

...EING IN THE DARK
...ght vision goggles give
...es the ability to see in very
... light. In total darkness an
...rared flashlight casts a bright
...ht upon the scene for anyone
...aring the goggles, but nothing
... be seen by the target. Most
...these systems work much
...e the image-forming tubes
...ed on television cameras.
...e tube converts photons (light
...rticles) from the camera lens
...o electrons (tiny, electrically
...arged particles). The electrons
...ed towards a phosphor screen,
...king a brilliant glow where
...y strike it. The screen forms a
...ghter copy of the original scene.

Strong harness
supports heavy
goggles

Side view of
night goggles

Rifle stock rests
against shoulder

...WK EYE
...ch surveillance work
...es on ordinary cameras
... lenses that any wealthy
...otographer could buy over the
...nter. However, this powerful
...mm telephoto lens was specially
...tted for use by Soviet border guards
... intelligence agents. With it, Soviet
...es could close in on a distant scene
... photograph agents at work.

ALL DONE WITH MIRRORS
Spies in 19th-century France used these
innocent-looking binoculars to keep a
watch on their opponents. One lens
produced the same view as an ordinary
pair of binoculars. The other was a
dummy. Behind it, an angled mirror
gave a perfect view of whatever was
happening to one side – while the spy
appeared to be staring straight ahead. A
similar device is still available today.
Disguised as a lens hood, it enables spies
to photograph subjects at their side,
while pointing the camera forwards.

Real lens

Focusing
wheel

Dummy
lens

Real lens in side

Hole for angled mirror

Bugs and taps

BEFORE YOU WHISPER "Tell me!" in a friend's ear, take a careful look around. Whispered words seem secret, but with bugs and wiretaps, spies can make sure that no conversation is really private. Bugs are hidden microphones, usually linked to radio transmitters, and like the insects they are named after, some are tiny. A spy who tunes a radio receiver to the correct frequency can hear every sound that reaches the bug, even if he or she is elsewhere. Telephone bugs or transmitters perform the same service each time a telephone is used. Tape recorders make it easy to monitor (check) wiretaps and bugs. When there is a sound, recording starts automatically; the tape stops after there have been a few moments of quiet.

SENDING...
A basic bug or transmitter can be very small indeed. This one is the size of a matchbox.

...AND RECEIVI
This pocket-sized receiver pi up signals from the bug (le relaying them to headphones tape recorder. The bug is a "qu plant" type, small enough to h behind a picture. Its battery las week or so. The bug is cheap enou to abandon – returning to coll it doubles the risk of discove

EMBASSY SEAL
A gift from the Soviet Union, this replica eagle seal of the United States decorated the U.S. embassy in Moscow. In fact, the seal housed an ingenious bug. Sound made a spring inside the seal vibrate. Spies in a nearby building were able to detect the vibrations and interpret the words that caused them by using radar.

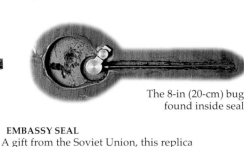

The 8-in (20-cm) bug found inside seal

CIA
microphone
wristwatch

WHAT IS THE TIME?
This CIA wristwatch conceals a microphone. It is normally inconspicuous, but in 1977, an American spy in Moscow betrayed himself because he had forgotten to remove his normal watch.

Link to tape recorder hidden in agent's clothing

PHONE-TAPPING
Telephone taps can be easier to place than bugs because spies need not enter the room they want to listen to. Unless there is a switchboard, a telephone tap can go anywhere between the telephone and the exchange. In this film reconstruction from *Stakeout*, Chris Lecce (played by Richard Dreyfuss) uses a wiretap to keep a vital witness in an organized crime case under surveillance.

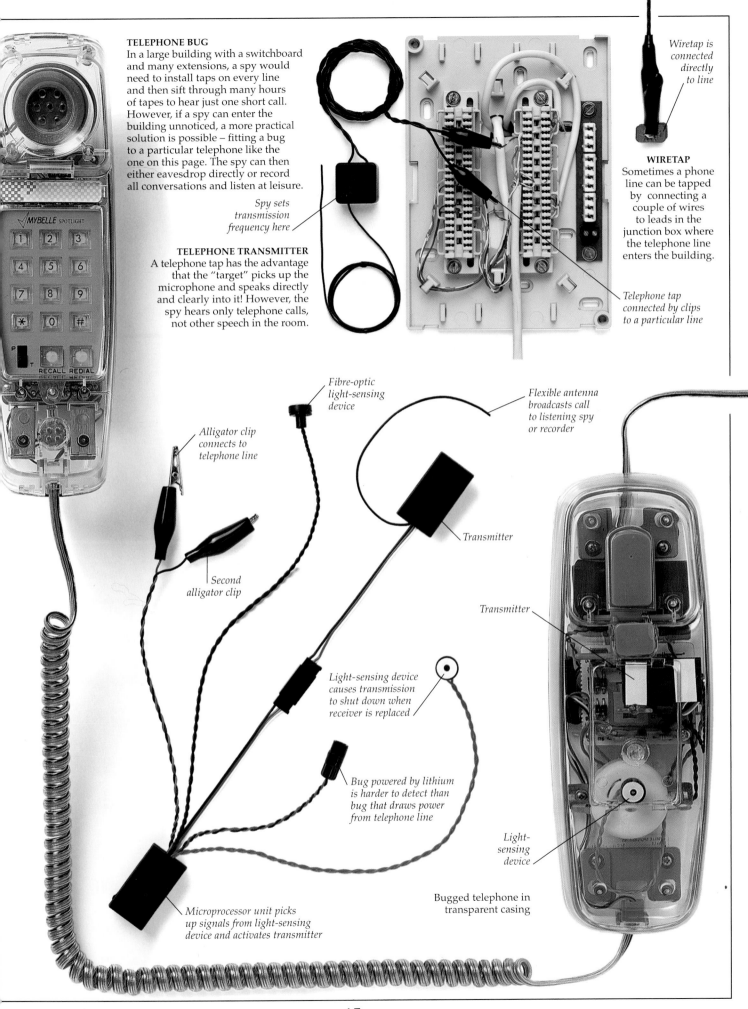

TELEPHONE BUG
In a large building with a switchboard and many extensions, a spy would need to install taps on every line and then sift through many hours of tapes to hear just one short call. However, if a spy can enter the building unnoticed, a more practical solution is possible – fitting a bug to a particular telephone like the one on this page. The spy can then either eavesdrop directly or record all conversations and listen at leisure.

Spy sets transmission frequency here

TELEPHONE TRANSMITTER
A telephone tap has the advantage that the "target" picks up the microphone and speaks directly and clearly into it! However, the spy hears only telephone calls, not other speech in the room.

Wiretap is connected directly to line

WIRETAP
Sometimes a phone line can be tapped by connecting a couple of wires to leads in the junction box where the telephone line enters the building.

Telephone tap connected by clips to a particular line

Fibre-optic light-sensing device

Flexible antenna broadcasts call to listening spy or recorder

Alligator clip connects to telephone line

Second alligator clip

Transmitter

Transmitter

Light-sensing device causes transmission to shut down when receiver is replaced

Bug powered by lithium is harder to detect than bug that draws power from telephone line

Light-sensing device

Microprocessor unit picks up signals from light-sensing device and activates transmitter

Bugged telephone in transparent casing

Listening in

Bugs do not have a very great range. In a city a spy must position a receiver within 2,625 ft (800 m) of the bug to be sure of good reception. Longer ranges are possible in rural areas, where buildings do not obstruct the signal, and where there is less interference from other radio users. The "listening post" – the receiving station – can be in an adjacent building, in a parked car, or even in the spy's pocket. The bug can be hidden in clothing if an agent has arranged a meeting with a contact in a street or park. Supporting agents listen in with cordless earphones.

Pin-sized antenna

Shirt hides induction loop

Receiver can switch between two different bugs

Tape runs continually throughout the conversation

BUG IN THE EAR

With a "necktie" of wire, an agent can monitor a bug without wearing conspicuous headphones. The listening device fits in the ear and looks like a hearing aid. The wire around the agent's neck creates an induction loop – a magnetic field that relays the amplified signal from a pocket receiver to the ear.

WEARING A WIRE

The radio signal from a bug hidden in a spy's clothing can alert counter-espionage agents operating bug detection equipment (pp. 48–49). A miniature tape-recorder gets around the problem because it does not broadcast a radio signal.

Wearer uses remote switch on microphone to turn tape off

A BETTER RECEPTION

Though some general-purpose receivers can pick up bug signals, specially designed units are often more convenient and provide better reception. This battery-powered model links up with a portable tape recorder for unattended monitoring. An agent who set it up to receive signals from a telephone tap would need to return to the device only occasionally to change the tapes.

Telescopic antenna

Socket for headphones

Car battery can power receiver for extended operation

Tape recorder can be hidden in briefcase

Tiny tape recorder looks like a personal stereo, but has been modified to provide far better sound quality

Bug is only 0.16 in (4 mm) thick, and can hide behind a credit card, or nestle between pages of a diary

STAKEOUT
Hidden microphones are legally used to investigate serious crimes and threats to national security. Here, the head of security for a large American corporation listens in on a suspicious conversation. Laws limit the use of bugs, but some citizens' rights groups fear the controls are too weak.

Compartments in spine of case conceal the power supply and transmitter electronics

Pocket calculator works normally, but broadcasts signal from sensitive microphone even while in use

Pen contains tiny bug

MAKING A CASE FOR BUGGING
Monitoring a meeting is a common task for both political and industrial spies. Business-people can have many reasons for recording conversations: tapes can provide evidence of unfair competition or help thwart a takeover by rivals. Bugging a briefcase is a discreet way to make a lasting record of "hush-hush" deals. Microphones built into an attaché case can pick up speech on the far side of a large room. The case can either record the conversation or transmit it to a monitoring device outside. Touching the lock and a brass rivet head at the same time activates the device. A bugged pen or calculator will attract no attention on a desk, and allows a spy to move the microphone nearer to the people talking.

19

Dropping in

HOMING PIGEONS have played an important part in intelligence work since the earliest days of espionage. Carrying a precious cargo of vital secrets, the homing pigeon can soar high over enemy territory. Roman general Julius Caesar (100–44 B.C.) used them to send intelligence messages during his campaigns in what is now France. Ever since, spies have valued the pigeon's speed and its ability to return home in almost any weather. More than half a million pigeons carried messages in World War I. Some even worked as spies – reconnaissance pigeons carried aloft tiny cameras to photograph enemy fortifications. In World War II, spies used pigeons to guide Allied bombers to the launch sites of the German V1 "flying bombs."

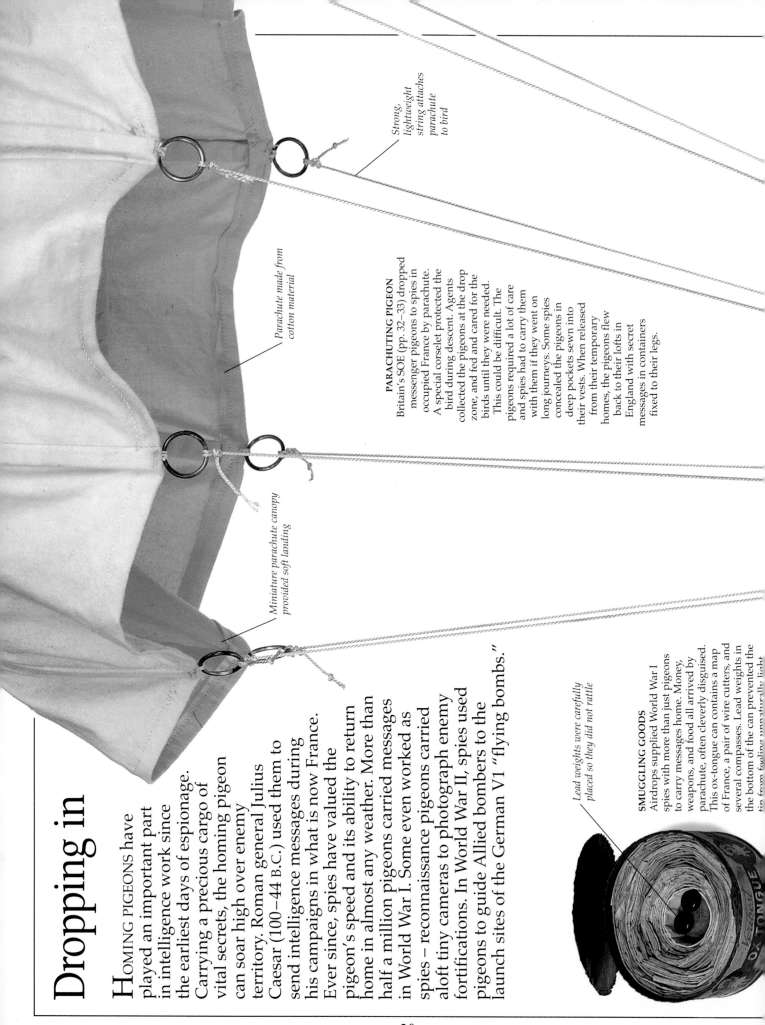

Strong, lightweight string attaches parachute to bird

Parachute made from cotton material

Miniature parachute canopy provided soft landing

PARACHUTING PIGEON
Britain's SOE (pp. 32–33) dropped messenger pigeons to spies in occupied France by parachute. A special corselet protected the bird during descent. Agents collected the pigeons at the drop zone, and fed and cared for the birds until they were needed. This could be difficult. The pigeons required a lot of care and spies had to carry them with them if they went on long journeys. Some spies concealed the pigeons in deep pockets sewn into their vests. When released from their temporary homes, the pigeons flew back to their lofts in England with secret messages in containers fixed to their legs.

Lead weights were carefully placed so they did not rattle

SMUGGLING GOODS
Airdrops supplied World War I spies with more than just pigeons to carry messages home. Money, weapons, and food all arrived by parachute, often cleverly disguised. This ox-tongue can contains a map of France, a pair of wire cutters, and several compasses. Lead weights in the bottom of the can prevented the tip from feeling unnaturally light

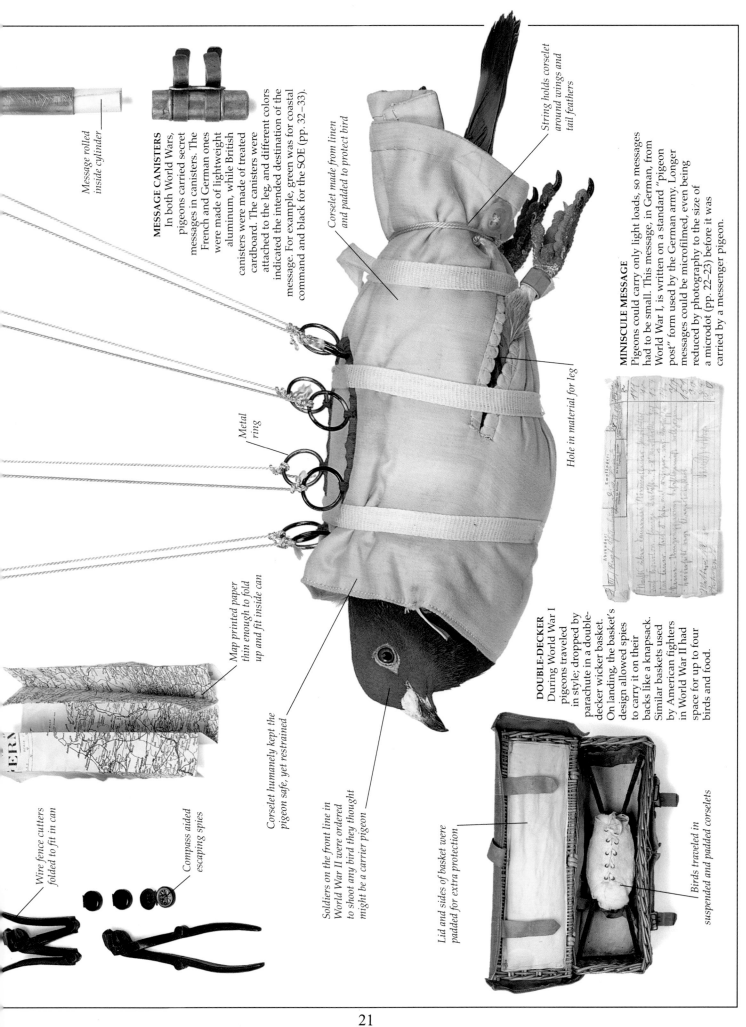

Message rolled inside cylinder

MESSAGE CANISTERS
In both World Wars, pigeons carried secret messages in canisters. The French and German ones were made of lightweight aluminum, while British canisters were made of treated cardboard. The canisters were attached to the leg, and different colors indicated the intended destination of the message. For example, green was for coastal command and black for the SOE (pp. 32–33).

String holds corselet around wings and tail feathers

Corselet made from linen and padded to protect bird

MINISCULE MESSAGE
Pigeons could carry only light loads, so messages had to be small. This message, in German, from World War I, is written on a standard "pigeon post" form used by the German army. Longer messages could be microfilmed, even being reduced by photography to the size of a microdot (pp. 22–23) before it was carried by a messenger pigeon.

Hole in material for leg

Metal ring

Map printed paper thin enough to fold up and fit inside can

Corselet humanely kept the pigeon safe, yet restrained

Wire fence cutters folded to fit in can

Compass aided escaping spies

Soldiers on the front line in World War II were ordered to shoot any bird they thought might be a carrier pigeon

DOUBLE-DECKER
During World War I pigeons traveled in style; dropped by parachute in a double-decker wicker basket. On landing, the basket's design allowed spies to carry it on their backs like a knapsack. Similar baskets used by American fighters in World War II had space for up to four birds and food.

Lid and sides of basket were padded for extra protection

Birds traveled in suspended and padded corselets

Secret messages

Spies rely on fast, secure communications. Speed is crucial because intelligence quickly loses its value, and secrecy is essential to protect both the messages sent and the spy. The invention of radio at the beginning of this century improved the speed of such communications, but not the security. With radios, spies could communicate over long distances almost instantly. However, anyone tuning to the right wavelength was able to intercept radio messages. With two receivers and suitable antennae, counterespionage agents could pinpoint the transmitter in minutes and capture the spy.

Headphones allowed agent to listen to broadcasts without others hearing them

Transmitter works on electricity or battery power

Apparatus packs into a suitcase and weighs 32 lb (14.5 kg)

Oluf Reed Olsen's code sheets

Headphone connector

Frequency dial

Voltage adjuster

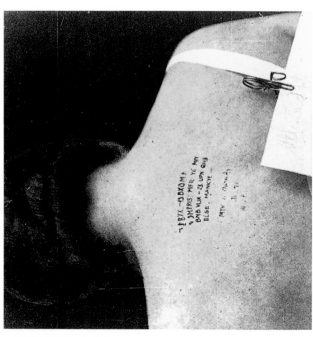

HUMAN SIGNALS
Spies sometimes take desperate risks to carry intelligence. This World War I courier carried a message written on her back in invisible ink. The ruse did not succeed: after the

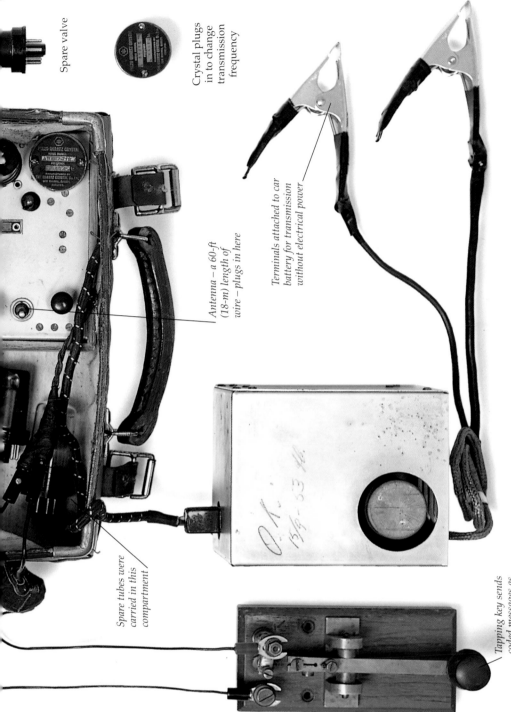

Spare valve

Crystal plugs in to change transmission frequency

Antenna – a 60-ft (18-m) length of wire – plugs in here

Terminals attached to car battery for transmission without electrical power

Spare tubes were carried in this compartment

Tapping key sends coded messages as long and short pulses of radio waves

NORWEGIAN SECRET AGENT

When German forces invaded neutral Norway in 1940, Oluf Reed Olsen fled the country in a sailboat. Reaching Britain, he trained as a radio operator, returning to Norway in 1943, where spies in the Kristiansand naval base supplied him with details of German shipping movements. Olsen coded the messages and transmitted them to Britain from a camouflaged camp hidden in the trees above the harbor at Kristiansand. He used the radio set shown here. The cipher was considered unbreakable because it was based on sets of random numbers of which Reed Olsen and MI6 held the only copies.

Oluf Reed Olsen using the Mark II suitcase radio at his camouflaged base in 1944

MICRODOTS
Photography provides agents with a simple way to send messages secretly. By photographing a document with a special camera, a spy can produce a microdot – a negative that is 300 times smaller than the original. This paragraph about microdots can be reduced to a microdot the size of a full stop, and then hidden in a perfectly innocent letter. The agent who receives the letter can read every word of the microdot with the help of a microscope.

Entire message can be reduced until it is the size of a period

CONVICTED BY RADIO
Peter and Helen Kroger hid a radio transmitter under the kitchen floor of their house. With it they transmitted British submarine secrets to Russia. They chose a house in west London, England, close to three busy airports, hoping that communications between aircraft and control towers would hide their secret signals. At their trial in 1961, the radio was used as evidence.

DOTTY PHOTOGRAPHY
Microdot cameras can be simple in construction and small enough to hide easily. However, microphotography is difficult to do. Unless agents are very careful with the exposure of the film and its processing, the dot will be impossible to read.

Microdot camera (actual size)

MICRODOTS
Photography provides agents with a simple way to send messages secretly. By photographing a document with a special camera, a spy can produce a microdot – a negative that is 300 times smaller than the original. This paragraph about microdots can be reduced to a microdot the size of a period, and then hidden in a perfectly innocent letter. The agent who receives the letter can read every word of the microdot with the help of a microscope.

Codes and ciphers

ESPIONAGE AGENTS use "codes" to communicate, and "ciphers" to keep their messages secret. In a code, letters, numbers, or symbols replace the words of a message or signal. Some codes are in general use. For example, when you mail a letter, a zip code guides it to the right destination. Spies sometimes send messages in Morse code – dots and dashes that all radio operators understand. Other codes are complicated and difficult to break. Ciphers provide further secrecy. They are similar to codes, but they have a secret "key" for encrypting the message – translating it into a cipher. The key can be a number, a word, even a poem. Anyone who has been given the key can easily decrypt the signal – change it back to plain text. Without knowing the key, the message reads as nonsense.

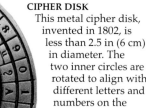

SIMPLE CIPHER
Ciphers do not need to be complicated if it is important only to hide their meaning from a casual glance. This jolly figure from World War I spells out "Ypres" (the site in France of a famous battle) and a date, the "8th."

CIPHER DISK
This metal cipher disk, invented in 1802, is less than 2.5 in (6 cm) in diameter. The two inner circles are rotated to align with different letters and numbers on the two outer circles. This produces a simple, easily broken substitution cipher in which each letter stands for another. "W," for example, represents "E" whenever it occurs.

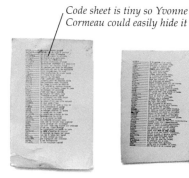

Code sheet is tiny so Yvonne Cormeau could easily hide it

CODE SHEETS
Charts like these make ciphers easy to write and hard to break. These miniature code sheets were hidden in the purse of SOE wireless operator Yvonne Cormeau in World War II (pp. 32–33). When she used a chart for Morse transmissions, a different letter would replace "E" each time it occurred in the message.

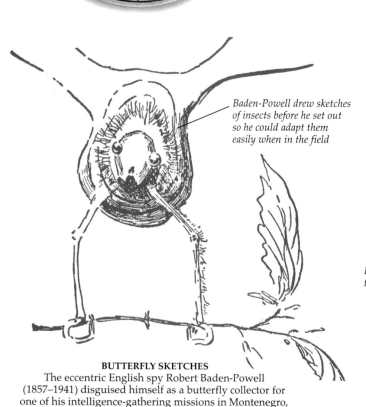

Baden-Powell drew sketches of insects before he set out so he could adapt them easily when in the field

BUTTERFLY SKETCHES
The eccentric English spy Robert Baden-Powell (1857–1941) disguised himself as a butterfly collector for one of his intelligence-gathering missions in Montenegro, on the coast of the Adriatic Sea. While he was there, he sketched this specimen of a moth perched on a twig.

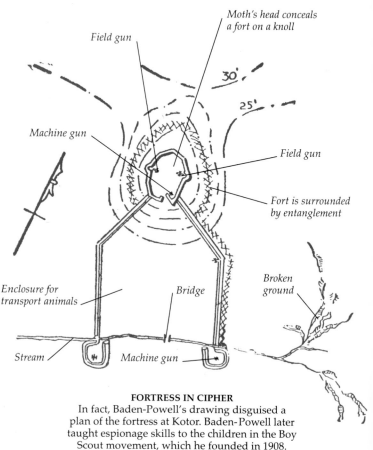

Moth's head conceals a fort on a knoll

Field gun

Machine gun

30'

25'

Field gun

Fort is surrounded by entanglement

Enclosure for transport animals

Bridge

Broken ground

Stream

Machine gun

FORTRESS IN CIPHER
In fact, Baden-Powell's drawing disguised a plan of the fortress at Kotor. Baden-Powell later taught espionage skills to the children in the Boy Scout movement, which he founded in 1908.

ROYAL CIPHER

...ry, Queen of Scots (1542–87) encrypted ...messages to allies outside her prison ...walls (pp. 28–29). In the substitution ...pher that they used, the same symbol ...ood for a letter each time it appeared, ...so that the cipher was easy to break.

Numbers between the symbols represented people's names

Coded letter signed by Anthony Babington, conspirator in a plot to assassinate Elizabeth I

...EDING UP ENCRYPTION

...e Enigma cipher machine was used by ...rman soldiers (above), diplomats, and ...es in the 1930s and during World War II. ...e signals baffled enemy cryptanalysts ...her experts) who intercepted them and ...d to break the cipher. The Polish secret ...vice, with the help of a recruited spy ...he German cipher office, was able to ...erpret three-quarters of the Enigma ...ssages by 1938, and in 1939, passed ...this knowledge to Britain and France.

Lid holds spare lightbulbs

Bulbs lit behind lettered windows on the lid to indicate enciphered character

Positions of rotors controlled encryption of each letter

Rotors spun after each letter, ensuring that cipher pattern was never repeated

Cipher was keyed in

Connecting sockets with plugs made the cipher more complicated

Rotors and plugs gave several billion combinations

Klappe
schließen

ENIGMA IN OPERATION

After setting plugs and three or four rotors, encryption on Enigma was automatic. Pressing a letter key lit up a different letter on the display above. The encrypted letter was different each time. Decryption on the receiving Enigma machine reversed the process. In principle, coded messages from the Enigma machine were impossible to read without knowing the rotor and plug settings. But that information and an actual Enigma machine supplied by the Polish Secret Service helped the British break most of the Enigma codes in an operation called "Ultra," which remained secret until 1972.

Intercepts and code-breaking

CIPHER CLERKS AT WORK
Britain's code-breaking center in World War II was at Bletchley Park near London. More than 5,000 employees there worked on up to 2,000 encrypted messages a day.

Cᴵᴾᴴᴱᴿˢ ʜᴇʟᴘ ᴘʀᴏᴛᴇᴄᴛ secret messages, but they do not destroy the meaning completely. Like a word puzzle, the sense of the message remains locked inside. An enemy who intercepts the signal will try hard to find the key. Intelligence agencies employ code-breakers called cryptanalysts to do this. With a substitution cipher (pp. 24–25), a cryptanalyst starts by counting letters. In English, "E" is used more often than other letters. So, if in the message "W" appears most, it probably stands for "E." The next step is to look for two-letter words ending in "E." There are only four in English: "he," "me," "be," and "we." Then the cryptanalyst will look for letters that stand on their own – in English there are just two one-letter words, "a" and "I." With techniques like these, and even more complex ones, cryptanalysts can solve elaborate cipher puzzles, although it can sometimes take them a long time. Computers speed the process, but cryptanalysts need to be very patient. Few, though, are as patient as a 17th-century Arab who deciphered a message to the sultan of Morocco. It took him 16 years.

ZIMMERMANN TELEGRAM
Deciphered in Britain in 1916, this telegram was sent by the Germans to their ambassador in Mexico. It suggested that Mexico form an alliance with Germany and invade three southern U.S. states. The interception of the telegram was possibly the most important spying event of the war. Shocked Americans quickly entered World War I on Britain's side.

Polish inventors named machine after the ice-cream "bombe" they were eating at the time

WRENS *(members of the Women's Royal Navy) operated the machines*

GOING LIKE A BOMBE
Cryptanalysts at the code-breaking center at Bletchley Park used some of the first computers to help them break codes and ciphers. In two hours, a "bombe" could try every combination of rotor positions that was in use on the simple Enigma machines that Germany was using until 1938. A later machine, called Colossus, was a forerunner of the programmable computers in use today.

Bombe simply stopped when it broke the cipher

The attack was at night and U.S. servicemen were asleep in their bunks

Unprepared U.S. technicians thought the Japanese planes were part of a training exercise

Japanese aircraft bomb Pearl Harbor, December 7, 1941

THE PURPLE MACHINE
Like Enigma (pp. 24–25), the Japanese Purple cipher machine used a plugboard to create a huge number of possible keys. However, Purple used telephone switches in place of the rotors found in Enigma. A team of U.S. cryptanalysts, including William Friedman (center left), cracked the Purple cipher by building a replica of the mechanism.

[PE]ARL HARBOR PREDICTED
[By] cracking the Purple code (right), American cipher [ex]perts predicted a Japanese attack on December 7, [194]1, but could not name the hour or the place. The [sp]ies Richard Sorge (pp. 34–35) and Dusko Popov [pp]. 56–57) had also warned of the air attack. American [pol]iticians decided to do nothing, and the devastating [sur]prise raid took place on Pearl Harbor in Hawaii. The [atta]ck killed 2,300 Americans, crippled the American [flee]t, and drew the United States into World War II.

[HU]SBAND AND WIFE TEAM
[Ru]ssian-born American William F. [Fri]edman (1891–1969) led the U.S. [Arm]y Signals Intelligence Service [tea]m that cracked Japan's Purple [cip]her. Friedman worked on ciphers [dur]ing both world wars. In the [192]0s, his wife Elizebeth broke [the] codes of rum smugglers [dur]ing Prohibition, when [alco]hol was banned [in t]he United States.

PIONEERING CRYPTANALYST
Herbert Osborne Yardley (1889–1958) was a brilliant cryptanalyst and pioneered code-breaking for the United States during World War I and afterward. He set up the U.S. unit that became known as the "Black Chamber" to read foreign intelligence material. His work in the 1920s was later used to help break the Purple cipher.

Herbert Yardley's security pass

THE "DEAD SOLDIER"
In 1943, the drowned body of a British [major] washed ashore in Spain. Papers he [w]as carrying described plans by the Allies [to] attack Greece and Sardinia, and German [troop]s immediately moved there. In fact, ["M]ajor Martin" was actually a civilian who [h]ad died of pneumonia. Intelligence chiefs [h]ad arranged for his body to be dressed as a soldier and pushed from a submarine off the Spanish coast. The Germans were completely fooled, and when they moved their troops, they left very few soldiers on Sicily – the Allies' real target.

Planted theater ticket stubs to make the major's identity appear genuine

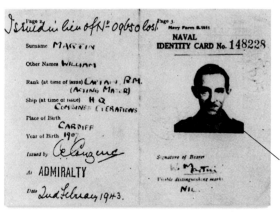

"Major Martin's" fake identity card planted by intelligence officers

Photograph of living person who looked like "Major Martin"

Concealment

SPY RING
Microdots (pp. 20–21) reduce documents to the size of a period. In World War II, British agents hid them in this hollow ring.

A CLOAK AND DAGGER are the symbolic trademarks of the secret agent. The spy hides the dagger, the badge of the assassin, under the cloak, which stands for secrecy, disguise, and concealment. Spies of the past could put on a cloak quickly to hide their true identity. Some chose more exotic disguises – Louis XV's agent the Chevalier d'Eon dressed as a woman for many years. For a modern spy, disguise is just as necessary, but much more subtle. Today's agents try to look ordinary, aiming to pass unnoticed in a crowd. Agents also choose ordinary-looking objects as hiding places for their surveillance equipment. Hidden in a working battery, a secret message is safe from even a close inspection. By miniaturizing their messages, spies can conceal them in even smaller objects. Large objects are more difficult to hide. However, an ingenious and determined spy can hide heavy equipment, tank engines – even kidnapped people.

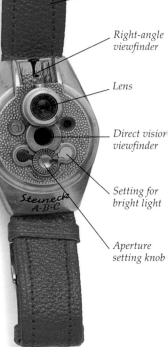

Wrist strap

Right-angle viewfinder

Lens

Direct vision viewfinder

Setting for bright light

Aperture setting knob

ROYAL BEER BARREL
Imprisoned by England's Queen Elizabeth I, Mary, Queen of Scots (1542–87) smuggled messages to sympathizers in a beer barrel. She wrapped encrypted documents in a waterproof bag, probably an animal bladder. Then she pushed the bag through the stopper hole into the barrel. Replies traveled back into her prison by the same route. Her "mailman," a double agent named Gilbert Gifford, betrayed the scheme (pp. 42–43).

Mary, Queen of Scots

Top hides 35 mm film

SMILE, PLEAS[E]
"Detective" cameras disguis[ed] as books, hats, and neckties fi[rst] appeared in the 1880s. As early [as] 1893 spies were taking pictu[res] with cameras shaped like pock[et] watches. This wristwatch came[ra] dates from 1948. On its 1-in[ch] (25-mm) diameter disk of film [it] takes eight pictures, each t[he] size of a little fingern[ail].

Cell provi[des] 1.5 volts pow[er]

Compartme[nt] is big enough [to] hold a roll of f[ilm]

Magnet grips base t[o] unscrew it

Wooden stopper seals barrel when full of beer

Spike pushes into ground

DEAD LETTER DROP
Many spies conceal messages in prearranged hiding places, or "dead drops." Leaving a message in a spike at a dead drop is safer than arranging to meet an agent.

BATTERIES INCLUDED
This ingenious hiding place look[s] like a normal battery, and a cell inside provides enough power t[o] light a bulb. However, there is a secret compartment at the base.

Dukes as Comrade
Piotrovsky

Dukes as an ailing
intellectual

Dukes as a bearded
worker

Dukes as an epileptic

*D'Eon complained that
he sometimes forgot
whether he was wearing
a woman's headdress
or a man's helmet*

*People even
made bets on
d'Eon's true sex*

A RELUCTANT WOMAN
The Chevalier d'Eon (1728–1810) was an expert fencer and lawyer. He began his career as a spy for French king Louis XV in 1756. He posed as a shy woman in the Russian court to gain the confidence of the Russian empress, and also worked as a double agent for the British. He lived in London as a female at the end of his life, and when he died many people were shocked to learn his real identity.

AGENT ST 25
Paul Dukes became an expert in disguise as head of British intelligence in Russia. He was in Moscow in 1917 when revolution swept the Communists to power. Pursued by the *Cheka* (secret police), Dukes cheekily posed as a Comrade Piotrovsky, a Cheka officer. To the British, he was "Agent ST 25."

*nps held
es and neck*

Small seat

HOW TO SMUGGLE A SPY
In 1964, drugged and bundled in a trunk, Israeli Mordecai Louk narrowly escaped being exported from Rome to Cairo disguised as "diplomatic mail." He was freed when a customs guard heard the box whimper. He had been spying in Italy for the Egyptians.

*Leather
slots for feet*

*Trunk was only
53 in (137 cm) long*

Spies at war

ADVANCING ARMIES rely on expert soldiers to survey the land ahead and judge the enemy's strength. However, not all are spies. Some are scouts who work openly and wear army uniforms. If they are caught, they spend the rest of the war in prison. Spies, on the other hand, disguise themselves to avoid capture, and they collect information secretly. Anyone caught in enemy territory wearing the clothes of a civilian can be tried as a spy, and the punishment – usually execution – is immediate. Despite this harsh penalty, spies have operated in almost every war. The 18th-century German king Frederick the Great even bragged about the number he employed. Mocking a French commander as a gourmet, he joked, "A hundred cooks follow him – but ahead of me go a hundred spies!"

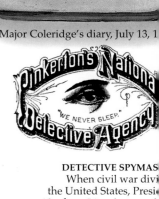

Major Coleridge's diary, July 13, 1

DETECTIVE SPYMAS
When civil war divi the United States, Presi Abraham Lincoln turned private detective to help ga intelligence for the Union a The choice seemed a natural o the Scotsman Allan Pinke (1819–84), head of the fam agency, had already foiled attempt to assassinate Linc Unfortunately, Pinkerton k little about war, and his ag were clumsy and someti cowardly. He resigne Lincoln's spymaster in 1

SOUTHERN BELLE
Many women worked as spies in the U.S. Civil War (1861–65), and Belle Boyd (1844–1900) became one of the most famous Confederate (Southern) agents. She learned military secrets from Union (Northern) officers lodged in her Virginia home, and braved gunfire to tell Confederate leaders. After capture and then release in a prisoner exchange, she received a hero's welcome in the South.

DEATH OF A SPY
Major John André, above, (1750–80) was hanged as a spy during the American Revolution (1775–83). He had gone to meet American traitor Benedict Arnold (1741–1801), the commander of West Point, a fortress that guarded the Hudson River Valley. Arnold wanted to surrender the fort to the British, and he handed André details of his plans. The ship that was to take André and the secret plans back to the British army was fired upon and left without him. André disguised himself as a civilian but was caught by American militia with the secret papers in his boots.

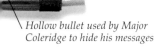

Hollow bullet used by Major Coleridge to hide his messages

~HTING THE BOERS

~he Boer War (1899–1902), British
~es fought to control farms and
~d in what is now South Africa.
~ir enemies were the Afrikaners,
~oers, descendants of white Dutch
~ers. Major H. F. Coleridge was
~ng those who spied for the British,
~ his diaries (left) record details of the
~r defenses. The British intelligence
~ice did not realize the value of the
~lligence that spies like Coleridge
~plied, and he had to plead for more
~ey to continue his work (below).

CARTOON CAPTURE
During World War I
(1914–18), spies usually
operated far from the front
line, in neutral nations
such as Switzerland and
the Netherlands (Holland).
Nevertheless, the public fear
of spies and their exploits
inspired many cartoons.
This colorful example shows
a German spy captured
by French troops.

Coleridge sent this telegram asking for more money in 1900

French-born Violette Szabo was the best shot in Britain's SOE

COURAGEOUS COMMANDO
Violette Szabo's only qualification when she applied to be a British
spy in World War II (1939–45) was her skill with a rifle – London
shooting galleries banned her because she always hit the target. She
became a spy to avenge the death of her husband, Etienne (above),
who died fighting for the British in North Africa. Admired by
fellow spies for her courage and determination, she was captured
after a gun battle on her second SOE (Special Operations Executive)
mission in France, when she was sabotaging telegraph lines.
Violette Szabo was executed in a German prison camp.

~oln (center)
~dismissed
~eneral

*On September 17, 1862,
12,000 Union troops died at the
battle of Antietam, largely
due to bad intelligence,
and Pinkerton
resigned*

TOO GOOD TO BE TRUE
The cleverest agent of World War II,
code-named "Cicero," was extremely
good at spying for Germany. He was
an Albanian and his real name was
Elyesa Bazna. While working as valet
to the British ambassador in Turkey,
he opened the embassy safe
and photographed secret codes,
lists of British spies, and the Allied
plans to invade Europe. But these
documents were so secret that the
German leaders could not believe
they were genuine and ignored
Cicero. Nevertheless, they paid
him a fortune in banknotes –
but all of them were forgeries.

A cover story

DISGUISED AS A CHILD'S NURSE, "Annette" passes through a wartime roadblock in southwest France. Annette, who is really the radio operator Yvonne Cormeau, tells her "cover story" well, escaping capture for a year and transmitting more than 400 coded messages. During World War II, the lives of many secret agents depended on their cover stories – invented pasts designed to hide their real identity. In Britain, the Special Operations Executive (SOE) gave trained agents cover stories that they learned by heart. Then the SOE dropped the agents in France by parachute or small boat.

BITTER PILL
All SOE agents carried a suicide L-pill, which would kill in five seconds. No agent ever used it.

Fake French matchbox

FOR DEFENSE
Male and female agents learned techniques of silent killing, and all carried knives to put the techniques into practice if necessary.

VITAL TIMING
A late arrival usually signaled danger. Cautious agents did not wait more than a few minutes at a rendezvous.

PARTING GIFT
SOE agents were given a valuable present such as this silver cigarette case before leaving on a mission. The gift could be used as a bribe if an agent was caught by a corrupt official.

MAPS
Agents used local maps to plan sabotage. A silk map (above) folds very small to aid concealment.

Wallet

Powder compact

Mirror

TINY TAPPER
A Morse code key was small enough to hide easily in a handbag.

PLUG-IN TUNING
Yvonne Cormeau carried a variety of crystals. She could change them to tune her SOE radio to the correct wavelength.

Code sheets

HANDBAG HIDING PLACE
Between the lining and outer skin of Yvonne Cormeau's handbag is the secret compartment in which she hid code sheets (pp. 24–25) and a transmission schedule.

SOE carefully removed all English labels before sending an agent into enemy territory

The clothes had to be tailored in the French style of the 1940s

...ry detail of clothing ...forced the cover story – ...agent posing as a clerk ...uld wear a simple, ...xpensive hat like this one

...nne Cormeau's ...tered leather ...efcase

Briefcase fitted in with one of Yvonne Cormeau's disguises – a district nurse

Yvonne Cormeau's dress was made from lightweight cotton

Stockings could be used as a bribe by the SOE agent, as silk was very rare in wartime

Suede shoes

YVONNE CORMEAU, SOE RADIO OPERATOR
Many of these items belonged to Yvonne Cormeau, the SOE agent whose cover name was Annette. She parachuted into France on the night of August 22, 1943 and worked as a radio operator. Her natural caution helped her avoid capture until Allied forces liberated France in 1944. On one occasion, she recognized another agent on a train but resisted the temptation to speak – she had learned in training that if he was under suspicion, they might both be captured. On the other hand, Yvonne Cormeau knew when it was worth taking a risk. Although most radio operators moved their radio sets daily to avoid capture, she felt safe transmitting from the same house for six months. From the windows she could spot interception vans over 3 miles (5 km) away.

Double agents and defectors

A TRAITOR'S DEATH
Japanese counterespionage agents unmasked Richard Sorge for their German allies. He was condemned and executed in 1944.

TRIBUTE TO A SPY
Richard Sorge (1895–1944) appeared to be a fanatical Nazi during World War II. While a political adviser to the German ambassador, he was feeding secrets to Germany's Russian enemies. Soviet stamps showed Sorge as a hero.

DOUBLE AGENTS ARE REALLY "controlled enemy agents." Rather than serving two masters they work for only one side in a war of espionage – but they deceive the other side into thinking they are working for them, and instead steal their secrets. Being a double agent is very risky. To be successful, they must develop the trust of an intelligence agency, while their sole aim is to betray that trust. If caught, they can expect no mercy in their punishment. Double agents may be volunteers, or they could be spies unmasked by counterintelligence agencies who have been "turned" (recruited and controlled) rather than prosecuted. Spies who are turned are especially valuable. Their new masters provide them with false but believable information, and the spy passes on the bogus secrets as if they were true, causing confusion and doubt. Spies who flee to the nation that was once the target of their spying are called "defectors." Although they may be admired in the country to which they are truly loyal, they earn just as much hatred in the country they betrayed.

Aldrich and Rosario Ames after their separate trials for spying

ANCIENT SPYMASTER
Chinese commander Sun Tzu was among the first to write about double agents. He called them "doomed spies," who "are deliberately given false information and told to report it to the enemy." Sun Tzu wrote his book, *The Art of War*, in the 4th century B.C.

RUSSIAN AGENT AT THE CIA
For nine years Aldrich Ames (born 1941) was a Soviet spy while working as a trusted officer at the CIA. Ames and his wife, Rosario, provided details of many spies recruited by the CIA, and with their help, Moscow was able to build a network of double agents who deceived their CIA bosses. The pair was paid well by the Russians for their treachery.

ЗДРАВСТВУЙТЕ, ТОВАРИЩ ФИЛБИ

«Если бы мне предстояло начать жизнь сызнова, я начал бы так, как...

Феликс ДЗЕРЖИНСКИЙ.

...ЕКАБРЬСКОЕ морозное утро, ночная мгла еще не ушла с заснеженных улиц. Деревья на Гоголевском ...аре покрыты пушистым инеем. У ...ейбусной остановки — цепочка по-

представить все, что угодно. Предположить, что в то августовское утро в кабинете за столом напротив него сидел кадровый сотрудник советской разведки, он не мог даже в дурном сне.

— Я делал, что мог в то время, и был счастлив узнать однажды, что я зачислен в кадры советской разведки.

— Каким же образом, товарищ Ким, вам удалось попасть на службу в английскую разведку?

— Это довольно длинная история, — говорит он. — После окончания Кэмбриджа я некоторое время работал в одной

— Я пошел вверх по служебной лестнице. Через год я уже был заместителем начальника одного из отделов МИ-6.

— МИ-6, что это значит?

— В Англии существует две службы: под кодовым названием МИ-5 скрывается контрразведка, МИ-6 — это собственно секретная разведывательная служба.

— Западная пресса отмечала, что ва...

Он был внимателен в обращении с людьми, но по существу относился к ним свысока. В дела он не вникал, и, я бы сказал, при всей его агрессивности он был дилетантом, о чем лучше всего говорит авантюра с вторжением на Кубу... Его позорно провалилась. Считали, что он занял этот пост благодаря своему брату — Джону Фостеру Даллесу.

HERO'S WELCOME
Philby escaped to Moscow from Beirut, where he had been working under cover as a journalist. The Soviet newspapers welcomed him with banner headlines. This one reads "Greetings, Comrade Philby."

...LD WAR DOUBLE AGENT
...rold "Kim" Philby (1912–88) ...ame a Communist while he was ...dying at Cambridge University, ...I was a Soviet spy by 1933. Yet, ...en years later he had a job with ...tain's MI6 intelligence service. ...er thirty years of spying, he fled ...Moscow. A grateful Soviet Union ...e him a pension and an apartment, ...office of which is shown above.

MEDALS FROM BOTH SIDES
Philby received this KGB badge soon after his arrival in Moscow. Later the Soviet Union awarded him the Order of the Red Banner. Eighteen years earlier, England's King George VI, unaware that he was a spy, had given Kim the Order of the British Empire.

Hammer and sickle, the symbol of the Soviet Union

Gordievsky wrote memoirs of his time in the KGB

RETIREMENT IN MOSCOW
After defecting, Philby lived in Moscow until his death in 1988. His son took this photograph of him in the 1970s. The treachery of Philby and his fellow spies Guy Burgess and Donald Maclean left behind a trail of mistrust. Their espionage discredited the British intelligence services.

SECURITY SECRETS
As head of the KGB mission in London, Oleg Gordievsky (born 1939) had access to the most sensitive information about his country's espionage activities. Secretly he despised the Soviet system and had been spying for the West since 1966. He defected to Britain in 1985, when his Soviet masters began to suspect him.

Gordievsky with his book, *KGB: The Inside Story*

SECRET IDENTITY
Igor Gouzenko (1919–82) was a cipher clerk in the Soviet embassy in Ottawa. He did not wish to return to the Soviet Union, and defected with evidence of ongoing Soviet spying. He was turned away as a crank by newspapers and government departments, but the Mounted Police believed and protected him. For this TV interview he wore a hood to keep his identity secret.

Secret weapons

ESPIONAGE HAS A BLOODY PAST. Spies were busiest in wartime, when there was danger everywhere; and when war ended, it was the job of intelligence organizations to make sure peace continued. Sometimes they used weapons to achieve this peacetime aim, and many wartime spies carried weapons openly. Others disguised their guns and knives in often ingenious ways. With the Cold War (pp. 38–39) came greater secrecy. Both Warsaw Pact and Western powers attempted killings, and some, like the murder of Georgi Markov, succeeded. Other schemes did not: apparently the CIA twice tried, and failed, to kill Cuba's president Fidel Castro with poison. The agency also considered more unusual weapons. They plotted to put deadly bacteria in Castro's cigar and to blow him up with an exploding clam while he swam in the sea. But not all the agency's weapons would have been fatal. The strangest plot just aimed to humiliate the Communist leader. By sprinkling a chemical powder in Castro's shoes, CIA agents planned to make his famous beard fall out!

Pushing the trigger near the handle fired the pellet

DEADLY PENCIL
Disguised as pencils, these two weapons were used in close combat. The stabbing pencil contains a cross-shaped blade, and the propelling pencil fired a single chromium-plated bullet. Agents of Britain's SOE (pp. 32–33) used them to gain a brief advantage, so that they could seize more powerful weapons from their opponents.

Pencil is cut away here to show knife inside

Shortened barrel

Gun no bar limit accur

Modified Webley & Scott 6.35 mm pistol

Georgi Markov in 1978

UMBRELLA KILLER
Bulgarian Georgi Markov broadcast criticism of his country's leadership from London. Walking home along a London street one day in 1978, Markov felt a sharp pain. He looked around to see a man picking up an umbrella. Markov quickly developed a fever and died three days later. His assassin, a Bulgarian agent, had used a specially designed umbrella to fire a tiny pellet containing a powerful poison into Markov. Ten days earlier, Bulgarian agents in Paris had attacked another opponent of the country's rulers, but the victim recovered.

Gas cylinder made umbrella work like air rifle

Holes in tiny pellet contained poison

Trigger guard

GUN BELT
Worn on a belt under clothing, this small World War II pistol had a very short range. To be sure of a direct hit, an assassin needed to be standing right next to the target. A firing cable from the belt's buckle passed down the sleeve of the coat that covered the gun. The great advantage was that a spy could pull the trigger without anyone seeing him or her take aim or fire.

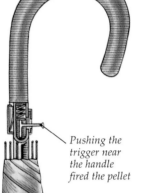

SIMPLE SLASHERS

ot all weapons were
ned at people. These
r-sharp knives were
designed to destroy
icle tires. They were
mall enough to hide
ily, yet with a single
slash an agent could
in valuable minutes
n which to make an
ape. Saboteurs used
knives to completely
mmobilize a vehicle
slashing all the tires
ncluding the spare).

*Knife hung
from thong
around neck*

*Small slasher
resembles ring*

RING REVOLVER

Concealed weapons
are nothing new.
The well-equipped
French spy of the 19th
century carried this
tiny revolver fixed to
a ring. By revolving
the chamber, the
agent could fire five
shots. Because of its
small size and firing
method, this design
was sometimes called
a squeezer pistol
or palm pistol.

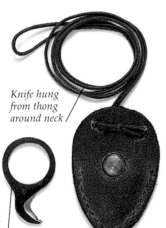

*Because the pistol
is so small, it had a
very limited range*

*The ring gun
can fire five bullets*

LETHAL GLOVE

Some spies' weapons
appear more dangerous to
the person using them than
to the victim. An agent
firing this ingenious "glove"
pistol had to take careful
aim, as its single bullet could
easily take off a couple of
fingers. The U. S. Office of
Naval Intelligence
produced the
gun for its
World War
II agents.

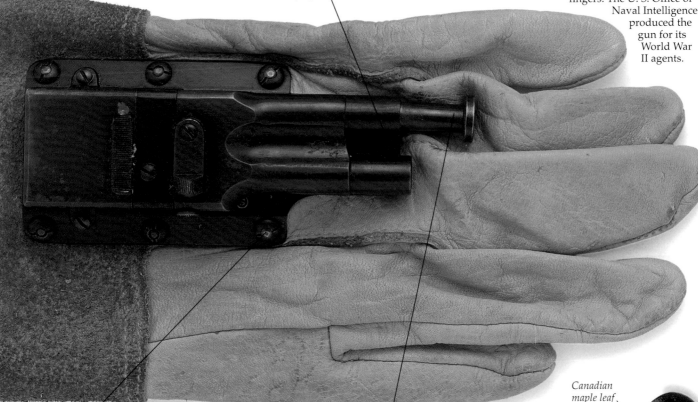

*Barrel poked out
between fingers*

*Pistol is riveted
to a leather glove*

*Pressing the barrel against
the victim's body fired the gun*

*Canadian
maple leaf*

*Concealed
blade*

Concealed blade

Concealed blade

*French
tricolor*

*Coin has a
hidden blade*

HEEL AND COIN BLADES

Despite their vicious appearance,
knives hidden in shoe heels were
not intended for attack. Instead, the
concealed blades allowed agents
who were tied up to cut themselves
free. Spies also hid knives in low-
denomination coins. They hoped
that enemy guards would let them
keep their loose change in their pockets –
even if the guards stole the paper money.

MESSY KNIVES

Wartime intelligence
agencies designed these
knives so they could be
hidden in a coat lapel or
cuff. A captured agent
could use a knife to attack
guards and escape. Instructors
who trained the spies warned that
the results were often "messy."

The Cold War

WHEN WORLD WAR II ENDED in 1945, the future looked bleak for secret agents. However, a golden age of espionage was about to begin. A political boundary split Europe in two. Nicknamed the "Iron Curtain," it was actually just a line on a map. To the east lay the Communist world – the Soviet Union and its allies – who wanted to create a classless society that shared everything. Nation to the west, supported by the United States, were capitalist, believing in the private ownership of property and businesses. Eastern and Western nations were deeply suspicious of each other, and their rivalry became known as the Cold War. Spies thrived in the atmosphere of mistrust that the Cold War created. They had plenty of work, with East and West racing to construct the biggest bombs, and each side sending spies to discover what the other side was plotting. And because of all this activity, each side needed more spies at home to catch enemy agents at work. On both sides of the Iron Curtain, fear of nuclear war mean that the money for spying never ran out. Finally, in 1989, the Cold War ended, and the process of reuniting Germany, which had also been split in two, began.

HUNT THE MISSILE
Missile bases are easy to spot on photographs from spy satellites (pp. 52–53), so the United States and the Soviet Union developed submarine-based missile launchers that could hide beneath the waves. The designers of this Trident missile claimed it would be used to hit missile bunkers. Opponents believed that cities would be the real targets.

Distinctive mushroom-shaped cloud

TESTING THE BOMB
The United States tested its atom bombs in the Nevada desert, far from the prying eyes of enemy spies. The power of these bombs to destroy civilization frightened everyone and may have gone a long way toward ensuring that neither side in the Cold War actually used one.

Crowds cheered as everyone wi a hammer and chisel chipped the wall

"KEEPING THE WORLD SAFE"
Politicians during the Cold War believed in "mutually assured destruction" (MAD). If each side had enough bombs to destroy the other, they reasoned, neither side would dare risk war. The two "superpowers," the Soviet Union and the United States, each built huge missiles with nuclear warheads. They never launched them. These American Titan II missiles are in storage, waiting to be converted into satellite launchers.

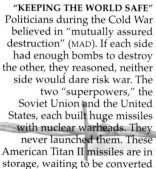

THE WALL DIVIDING EUROPE
Cold War espionage was most intense in Berlin, the capital of East Germany. Berlin was situated well inside East Germany, but a wartime treaty gave France, Britain, and the United States control of West Berlin, so the city was itself divided into West and East. To prevent refugees from escaping to the West across the new border, the East Germans divided the city of Berlin with a wall in 1961. The destruction of the wall in 1989 united Germany and symbolized the end of the Cold War.

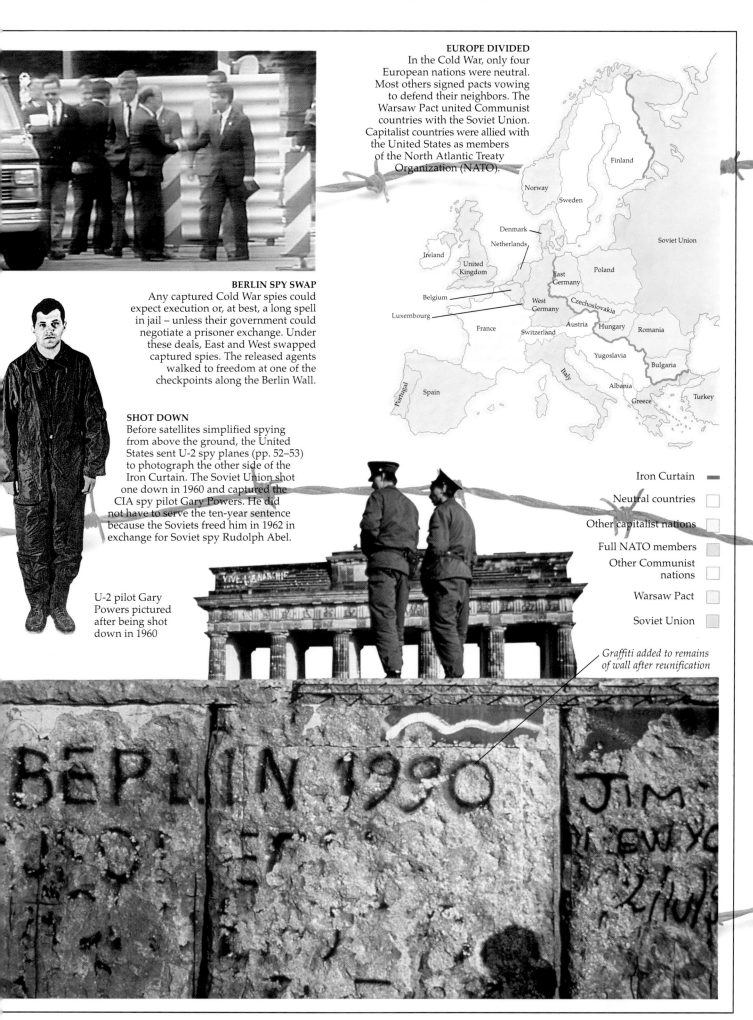

EUROPE DIVIDED
In the Cold War, only four European nations were neutral. Most others signed pacts vowing to defend their neighbors. The Warsaw Pact united Communist countries with the Soviet Union. Capitalist countries were allied with the United States as members of the North Atlantic Treaty Organization (NATO).

Finland

Norway

Sweden

Denmark

Netherlands

Ireland

United Kingdom

Soviet Union

East Germany

Poland

Belgium

West Germany

Czechoslovakia

Luxembourg

France

Austria

Hungary

Romania

Switzerland

Yugoslavia

Bulgaria

Portugal

Spain

Italy

Albania

Greece

Turkey

BERLIN SPY SWAP
Any captured Cold War spies could expect execution or, at best, a long spell in jail – unless their government could negotiate a prisoner exchange. Under these deals, East and West swapped captured spies. The released agents walked to freedom at one of the checkpoints along the Berlin Wall.

SHOT DOWN
Before satellites simplified spying from above the ground, the United States sent U-2 spy planes (pp. 52–53) to photograph the other side of the Iron Curtain. The Soviet Union shot one down in 1960 and captured the CIA spy pilot Gary Powers. He did not have to serve the ten-year sentence because the Soviets freed him in 1962 in exchange for Soviet spy Rudolph Abel.

U-2 pilot Gary Powers pictured after being shot down in 1960

Iron Curtain	▬
Neutral countries	☐
Other capitalist nations	☐
Full NATO members	▨
Other Communist nations	☐
Warsaw Pact	☐
Soviet Union	▨

Graffiti added to remains of wall after reunification

VIVE L'ANARCHIE

BERLIN 1990

JIM

Spymasters

INTELLIGENCE CHIEFS HAVE enormous influence. Their access to valuable and secret information means that the few chiefs who choose not to serve their country wisely have dangerous powers. Usually chiefs, or spymasters, take orders from a trusted government group, but often this group does not know what the spies are really doing. In the past, spymasters in Europe received their orders directly from the king or queen. However, in 1519 a Venetian diplomat wrote of the English king Henry VIII' first spymaster, Cardinal Wolsey, that he "rules both king and the entire kingdom." In this century, until the Cold War ended, secret service chiefs controlled whole Eastern European nations. J. Edgar Hoover's powers grew so great while he was the FBI chief that he was in a position to blackmail some of the most influential politicians in the United States. Countries are now more open about the existence of their security services, but the identity of agents in the spy networks is still a closely guarded secret.

ROMAN SOLDIER
General Scipio Africanus Major (236 – 184 B.C.) was among the most clever spymasters of the Roman Empire. While attacking the Spanish city of Carthago Nova, his spies discovered that the enemy's reinforcements were ten days' march away. As a result, the army and navy under Scipio's leadership won an easy victory.

POWER BEHIND THE THRONE
Cardinal Wolsey (1475–1530) became the most powerful man in England as the first head of intelligence services for King Henry VIII. Wolsey's agents opened the mail sent to diplomats from Venice and other nations. To protect their secrets, the ambassadors began to write their letters in code.

Wolsey had influence over the powerful Henry VIII for many years

INDIAN INTELLIGENCE
Mughal ruler Akbar (1542 –1605) united India. As a young king, he used fakirs (holy men) as spies. During his reign (1556–1605), Akbar extended the Indian empire and reformed the government. To do this he relied on intelligence reports provided by *kotwal* (local officials), who had a duty to employ spies.

INVISIBLE SPIES
The warring princes of 12th-century Japan used ninja as spies and silent assassins. The ninja got their name from the Japanese word meaning "to make yourself invisible." They were trained to high standards of fitness and were masters of disguise. One warlord, Takeda Shingen, so feared them that he fitted a second door to his bathroom to make escape easier.

RUSSIAN SECRET SERVICE
The first Tsar of Russia, Ivan IV (1530–1584), richly deserved his nickname "the Terrible." He ruled with the help of ruthless secret agents called the *Oprichniki*. Officially security police, the Oprichniki were really thugs who terrorized whole cities, killing and torturing without fear of punishment. They wore an emblem of a dog's head and a broom, symbolizing their power to sniff out and sweep away treason.

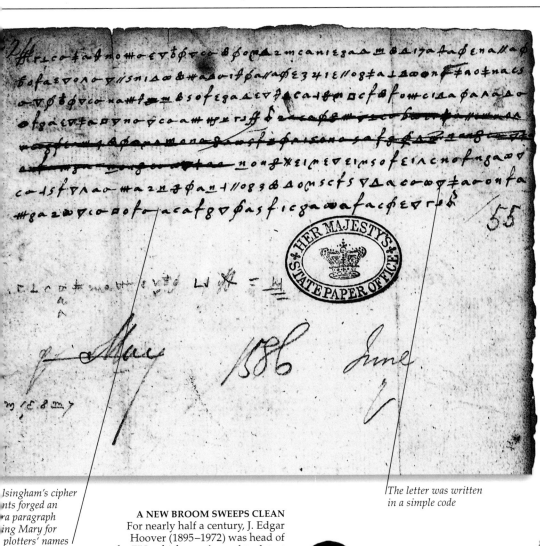

FATHER OF THE SECRET SERVICE
Francis Walsingham (c. 1532–1590) did much to build up the English intelligence service. His greatest achievement was to uncover a plot to murder England's queen, Elizabeth I. Walsingham's agents intercepted coded letters between the plotters and the queen's imprisoned cousin, Mary, Queen of Scots. The letters proved that Mary was involved, and she was executed in February 1587.

Isingham's cipher nts forged an a paragraph ing Mary for plotters' names

The letter was written in a simple code

A NEW BROOM SWEEPS CLEAN
For nearly half a century, J. Edgar Hoover (1895–1972) was head of the FBI, which was formed to detect enemy spies at work in the United States. But Hoover's agents also snooped on the private lives of politicians, including the president. By threatening to make sordid secrets public, Hoover clung to his enormous power. In 1947, the CIA was formed to deal with foreign security, and the power of the FBI was curbed.

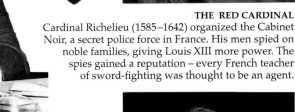

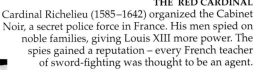

THE RED CARDINAL
Cardinal Richelieu (1585–1642) organized the Cabinet Noir, a secret police force in France. His men spied on noble families, giving Louis XIII more power. The spies gained a reputation – every French teacher of sword-fighting was thought to be an agent.

DOUBLE AGENT AT THE TOP
Alfred Redl (1846–1913) was Austria's chief spycatcher. He modernized the Austrian Secret Service but ran up huge personal debts. When Russia offered him money for vital information, he accepted and worked with them for ten years. Redl was accused of being a traitor in 1913 and shot himself rather than stand trial.

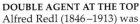

WOLF IN SHEEP'S CLOTHING
"The man without a face" was Markus Wolf's nickname during the Cold War. He was in charge of foreign operations for East Germany's Stasi (secret police). Wolf managed highly effective spy rings in the West. Even one of the close aides of the West German chancellor, Willy Brandt (b. 1913), had been recruited and was a Stasi spy.

The secret services

BEHIND EVERY SPY is a vast network for gathering intelligence. Organizations like the CIA and MI6 give spies documents, money, and help, and interpret the intelligence that the spies collect. The intelligence networks analyze information not only from human spies but also from a host of other sources. Satellites provide some of their data, and interception of radio signals supplies more. Many of their staff do nothing but read foreign newspapers, magazines, and journals. A clever analyst can learn much from these "open sources." During World War II, Russian intelligence experts noticed the United States was hoarding silver for "scientific research," and had banned all atomic physics journals. Without putting agents' lives at risk, they guessed – correctly – that the United States was developing an atom bomb.

SPY VS SPY
Mad magazine's cartoon figures made fun of secret service rivalry at the height of the Cold War.

BEWARE OF SPIES
The Republic of China has a large but highly secretive intelligence network. There is a Central Control of Intelligence that collects information, relying on different government organizations as well as the ordinary person in the street. In the 1970s, plaques such as this one (left) were posted all over the country to warn citizens against the activities of spies. Outside China, spies are believed to operate through the country's embassies and the New China News Agency.

Message reads: "At all times protect {our} secrets {and} everywhere guard against spies"

Emblem of the CIA

GUARDIANS OF THE UNITED STAT
The Central Intelligence Agency (CIA) h collected and analyzed foreign intelligence for t United States since 1947. It is also responsible f counterintelligence abroad. The less well-know National Security Agency, which is under t control of the Federal Bureau of Investigati (FBI), is actually bigger than the CIA a handles signal intelligence – codes, ciphe and the interception of communications. separate organization, the U.S. Secret Servi has responsibility for protecting the preside

REGNUM DEFENDE

Badge of MI5, the counterespionage agency in Britain

THE STASI
Until East and West Germany were reunited in 1990, the Stasi (State Security) controlled espionage for the East. East Germans had good reason to fear the Stasi. It employed more than 85,000 people and had detailed files on a third of the population.

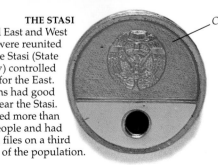

Copy camera with Stasi insignia

SECURITY STAR
Britain has twin security agencies to handle intelligence and counterintelligence at home (MI5) and abroad (MI6). In 1992, Britain was the first country to appoint a woman, Stella Rimington, as the head of a major intelligence agency. Until 1995, she was director of MI5, also called the Security Service, and originally formed in 1906. MI6 is the military name for the Secret Intelligence Service, and staff refer to its shadowy director as "C."

Badge worn by
a KGB agent

Map showing
the Soviet Union

ISRAELIS SPYING ABROAD
Israel has developed ruthlessly efficient security and intelligence services. Formed in 1949, Mossad (the Institution for Intelligence and Special Services) is responsible for foreign espionage and taking action against the country's enemies. Shin Beth (Security and Counterespionage Service) handles internal security.

A menorah – the symbol of Judaism

Badge of Mossad

SPYING IN RUSSIA
The KGB (Committee of State Security) controlled intelligence and counter-intelligence both inside the Soviet Union and overseas from 1954 until the 1980s. KGB agents also handled internal security, and the head of the organization had immense political influence. With the birth of modern Russia, the duties of the KGB were transferred to less powerful organizations in the new republics.

Vanunu's desperate message about his kidnapping in Rome

MOSSAD AT WORK
Agents of Mossad are particularly skilled at undercover work in foreign countries. When Mordechai Vanunu, a senior Israeli nuclear technician, revealed that Israel was building atom bombs, Mossad agents kidnapped him in Italy and took him back to Israel to face trial and imprisonment. While in Israeli custody, Vanunu wrote a message for the press on his hand, giving details of the kidnapping.

TARGET PRACTICE
The secret intelligence organizations of all countries deny that their agents carry out political killings. However, history proves this is not true. The CIA was famous for the actions it took against foreign leaders who opposed the United States – they hired Mafia killers to try and assassinate Cuba's Communist president, Fidel Castro (pp. 36–37). And the KGB defector Oleg Gordievsky claims that the KGB provided the poisoned umbrella that killed Georgi Markov (pp. 36–37).

DGSE agents abroad defend themselves with automatics like this

Manurhin
7.65 mm
pistol

PROTECTING FRANCE
Like many other nations, France divides its intelligence work among several organizations. The Direction Générale de la Sécurité Extérieure (DGSE) collects foreign intelligence and organizes counterintelligence abroad. The efficient Direction de la Surveillance du Territoire (DST) is controlled by the Ministry of the Interior and handles internal security. In the early 1980s, the DST was directly responsible for the expulsion of 47 Soviet diplomats suspected of spying.

Surveillance at work

Spies may be watching you. Business secrets are potentially valuable t[o]
rival companies, and to obtain those secrets, subterfuge is often used by
employees or outside agencies. To steal documents, industrial spies use
the tools and methods of a secret agent, and in order to protect those
documents from snoopers, businesses must adopt counterespionage
tactics (pp. 48–49). The devices shown here could all be used to protect
office secrets against intruders. However, all of them can also monitor
employees, for the espionage threat may come from inside the company[.]
Workplace spies watch low-paid staff
who may be bribed to sell information
to rivals. They aim to catch disgruntled
managers erasing computer disks. Even
office gossip is a target for hidden
microphones: it may warn that
staff members plan to leave
and set up in competition.

ARE YOU RECEIVING ME?
Businesspeople can learn a
lot about their clients with a
tiny bug like this. A sales
representative making a
presentation can "accidentally"
leave a bugged folder in the
conference room to record a
client's private conversation.

TAKING PICTURES
Professional spies might use an expensive came[ra]
like this Minox to photograph information.
However, the office photocopier is more of a
security threat. Employees do not arouse suspici[on]
if they use it – and the copies cost them nothing[.]

BUGGING THE WORKPLACE
An office appliance such as a
fluorescent desk lamp is an ideal
hiding place for bugs (above). It has
a built-in power supply and it sits in
the middle of the desk, so it is well
placed to pick up conversations.
Bribing someone to insert the bug
when equipment is sold is less risky
than entering the office to plant it.

*With a cheap modem, spies
can hack into insecure
computer networks
and copy data files*

*Base of desk lamp
is large enough
to conceal bug*

LOUD AND CLEAR
A sales representative who
has planted a bug is able to
eavesdrop on his client from
a car parked outside. By
pulling up the radio antenna,
he can pick up the signal and
listen to any discussion of the
sales pitch. The following
day, the sales rep can return
to negotiations, able to use
the information to change
strategy, and in a better
position to bargain.

*Shredded
paper*

PINHOLE PEEPER
More than one in every ten
American companies use video
cameras to spy on their employees.
Concealing the cameras is simple:
the smallest have lenses that are
smaller than a match head.

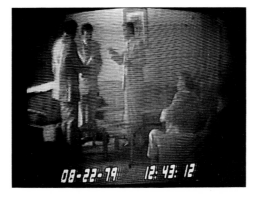

CAUGHT ON CAMERA
FBI agents used a hidden video camera in 1979
to collect evidence in a corruption case that they
nicknamed "ABSCAM." The video (above) proved
that members of the U.S. Congress were taking
bribes. Seven members of Congress were
convicted and went to jail.

INFINITY RECEIVER
Most office bugs have a limited range, but
infinity receivers use the telephone lines to
allow eavesdropping from any telephone in
the world. The "spy" must first install the
device, usually attached to the telephone
line. The bug operates when the spy dials
the number of the bugged telephone, then
presses a specially selected key on a touch-
tone telephone. The bug detects the tone
and stops the target phone from ringing.
Then it allows the spy to hear a
conversation in the room, with the
telephone mouthpiece acting as
a microphone. With the infinity
receiver, it is possible for someone in
Sydney, Australia, to eavesdrop on
conversations in Washington, D.C.

*Screwheads
on clock can
conceal camera*

*Tiny transmitters can
be hidden anywhere –
even in potted plants*

*innocent desk
essory can
ly hide a bug*

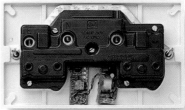

BUG IN A PLUG
Disguised as a wall socket, a bug is
impossible to detect without taking
the socket apart or using special
equipment. The socket functions
normally and also supplies the bug
with power. Some devices work like
baby alarms, using the mains power
cables – instead of radio waves – to
transmit signals. The spy monitors
any conversations with a suitable
receiver plugged into any other
socket on the same circuit.

*Infinity tape storage (above) records
phone calls and plays them back
when the "spy" dials in*

LKING RUBBISH
tting up documents does
necessarily destroy them.
termined industrial spies
painstakingly piece
ether shredded secrets.

Industrial espionage

GOVERNMENTS AND POLITICIANS are not the only targets of espionage. Businesses also have secrets that industrial spies try to steal or copy. This kind of espionage is rapidly expanding, but it is hardly new. The silk industry was an early victim. Until the 6th century, only the Chinese knew how to make this luxurious cloth. Then the Byzantine emperor Justinian I (483–565) used espionage to steal the secret of its production. He encouraged two monks to smuggle silkworms out of China in hollow canes. Industrial spying is more sophisticated today, but governments still encourage it if their nation benefits. In 1989, the French Department of Commerce planned to steal trade secrets from American and British companies. The spying became public when an informer mailed their "shopping list" to the CIA. Usually, though, it is businesses that use industrial espionage against their competitors. Successful spies find design details, lists of suppliers and buyers. Even advance knowledge of a price list can help squeeze a competitor out of business.

SPYING ON THE COMPETITION
One of the most common forms of industrial espionage is for trusted employees to quit and join a competitor – taking secrets with them. General Motors (GM) suspected José Ignacio Lopez de Arriortua of doing this when he left to join their rival Volkswagen. GM claimed that de Arriortua and other executives stole thousands of photographs and plans of the Opel Vectra, which was then secret. The car is now on the market.

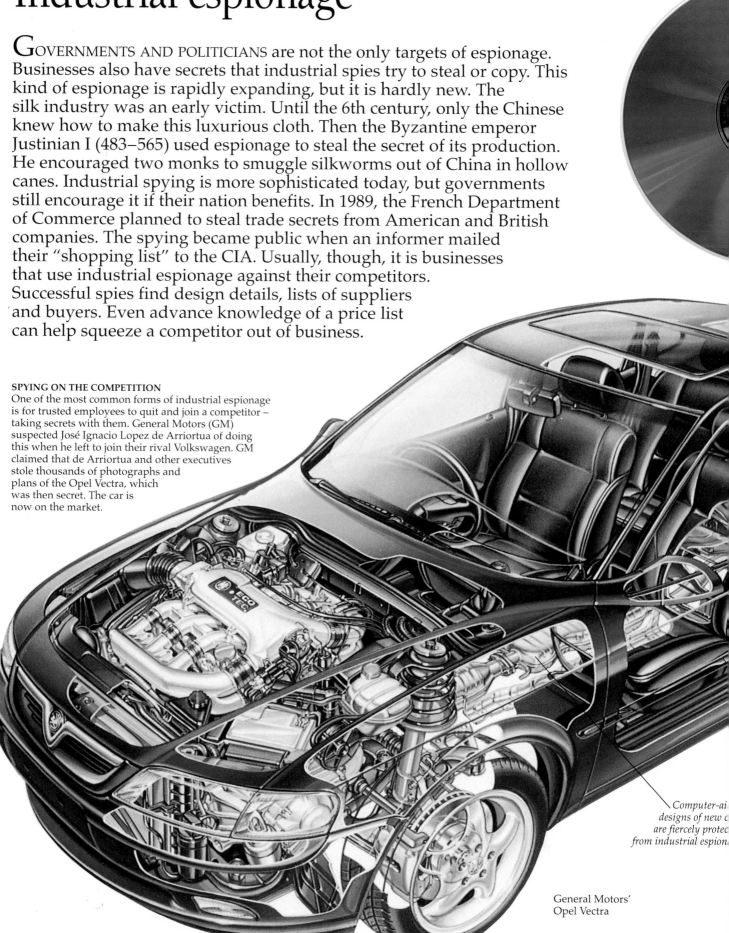

*Computer-ai
designs of new c
are fiercely protec
from industrial espion*

General Motors'
Opel Vectra

46

In the U.S. and Canada, annual losses in software, audio-tapes, and videos are $3.131 billion

Long before they emerge on the catwalk, designs of evening dresses are the target of spies

THE ENTERTAINMENT INDUSTRY

Piracy (illegal copying) and industrial espionage cut the profits made by people in the world of entertainment. From a single original, pirates can make millions of CDs or videos. Security at recording and film studios must be intense to make sure that master tapes are protected until the scheduled release date. Despite these precautions, industrial spies occasionally succeed in smuggling out a recording: pirates in Singapore made thousands of video copies of the James Bond film _A View to a Kill_ and distributed them throughout Asia before the film's London première.

To keep the shape of a new car secret, it can be disguised by fitting new parts in old car bodies when being road-tested

Revolutionary disk braking systems may interest rival car manufacturers

COSTUME DRAMA

Theft of ideas and designs in the fashion industry is big business. It is easy to claim and often difficult to prove. Cutters and other workers in the garment trade might copy patterns and sell them to another designer. It is also possible to re-create designs from sketches or photographs taken at designer dress shows.

COMPUTER SPYING

In 1981, the FBI caught a computer engineer, Kenji Hayashi, with secret details of IBM computer disk drive technology. His employers, Japan's Hitachi corporation, gave him more than half a million dollars, which he used to bribe IBM employees. After his arrest and trial, Hitachi had to pay IBM 60 times this sum in compensation.

INDUSTRIAL DIAMONDS

An industrial spy at General Electric earned $1 million a year for passing secrets of synthetic diamond manufacture to a South Korean company. By stealing the knowledge they needed to build a plant, the Koreans avoided paying license fees for the technology, and in this way saved the enormous expense of funding a research and development program. General Electric discovered the espionage in 1992.

Tiny synthetic diamonds in drill's tip help it cut faster

Counterespionage

I<small>N THE PAST</small>, bugging equipment was often simple, and wires from hidden microphones sometimes led directly to the eavesdropping spies. Today, finding bugs and wiretaps – and spies who use them – is harder. It is the job of counterespionage, or counterintelligence, agencies to track them down. However, detection of spies does not always lead to their capture – sometimes an enemy spy is more valuable if allowed to carry on as normal. Working spies can provide a counterespionage agency with useful information, especially if they do not know they are being watched. A spy's activities can reveal an enemy's intelligence requirements and give away secrets about spying techniques and equipment. These details can be used to help trap other spies. Counterintelligence services also use unmasked spies to feed false information to their enemies. Sometimes, by confronting spies with evidence of their guilt, a counterespionage agency can "turn" the spies, forcing them to work against their original masters as double agents.

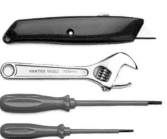

SOMEONE IS WATCHING YOU
Counterespionage agencies use many of the same tools as the spies themselves. This 19th-century cartoon makes fun of the craze for hidden cameras among spies and counterspies alike.

KEEPING CALLS SECRET
Devices called scramblers are sometimes used to keep telephone calls private. A typical scrambler chops speech into short segments, then rearranges these into an apparently random order for transmission along the telephone line. The "receiving" scrambler reverses the process. The people talking both use a scrambler, and they hear each other perfectly – but a spy who taps the line hears nothing but "gray noise" (a meaningless jumble).

Scrambler attached to telephone

SETTING THE CODE
The caller uses a row of tiny switches to set his or her scrambler to the same prearranged code as the receiving scrambler.

COUNTERSPY'S TOOL KIT
When checking for bugs, the counterspy uses screwdrivers and other basic tools to undo outlets and look behind light sockets and in other likely places. A visual inspection can reveal damage left when a bug was installed. By comparing cables with a wiring diagram, a counterspy can tell whether there are any other cables linking microphones to a distant transmitter.

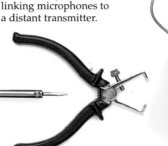

Rising tone in headphones indicates presence of a bug

Handle is removable to aid search of cramped spaces

Reducing power output helps pinpoint hidden bug

Probe detects bugs even when they are not transmitting

A NEW BROOM
This device is used by a counterespionage agent to quickly sweep (check) a room for bugs. The probe gives off a radio signal, which energizes semiconductor devices, such as transistors or integrated circuits. This creates a tell-tale signal that the "broom" detects. Innocent electronic devices such as telephones will activate the detector, but once these are taken into account, any remaining signals probably come from a concealed bug.

Strength
of signal

20 MHz

Frequency

12 MHz

...aks indicate
...ere there is a bug

WHICH ROOM IS BUGGED?

By displaying many scans from a tuned receiver in three-dimensional form, a room that contains a bug is revealed. The graph plots signal strength and frequency in megahertz for each room of a building.

LOOKING AROUND CORNERS

Many offices have large spaces under the floor, above the ceiling, and within the walls. These cavities are big enough to hide sophisticated and bulky monitoring equipment. To check such hiding places, counter-surveillance staff use small mirrors and tiny lights. Flexible goosenecks on the handles allow the searcher to insert the mirror deep inside inaccessible places.

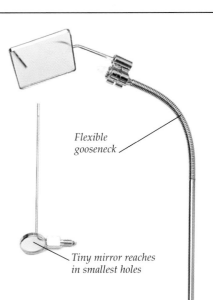

Flexible gooseneck

Tiny mirror reaches in smallest holes

Batteries in the handle power lamps

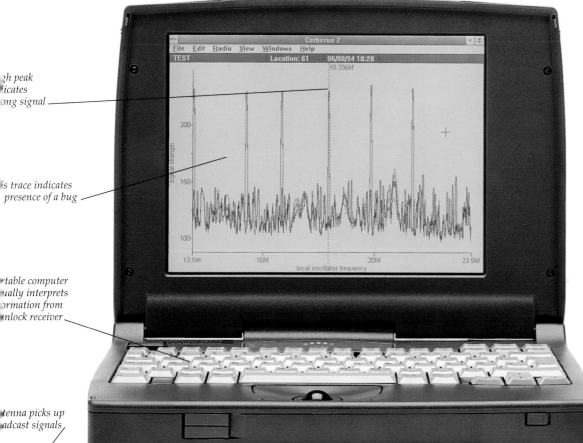

Cerberus 2

File Edit Radio View Windows Help

TEST   Location: 61   06/08/94 18:28

18.336M

signal strength

200

150

100

13.5M   16M   20M   23.5M

local oscillator frequency

...gh peak
...icates
...ong signal

...s trace indicates
...presence of a bug

...rtable computer
...ually interprets
...ormation from
...nlock receiver

...tenna picks up
...adcast signals

Device makes high-pitched sound if it detects a bug

SCANLOCK DETECTOR

Detecting cheap bugs is easy: play music in the suspect room, then use a radio receiver to scan commonly used frequencies. If you hear the music on the receiver there is a bug transmitter in the room. More sophisticated bugs broadcast on unusual frequencies or scramble their signals. This Scanlock wide-coverage tuned receiver picks up these "smart" bugs by scanning all the transmission frequencies within minutes.

BUGS ON DISPLAY

Connecting the Scanlock receiver to a portable computer displays its output in visual form. The jagged lines (trace) give a skilled operator detailed information about radio signals in the surrounding area. Higher peaks indicate stronger signals. Each trace forms a picture of radio signal activity at one particular time. If a bug then switches on, its signal will change the shape of a later trace.

Signal strength meter leads operator to bug

PINPOINTING A BUG

Once counterespionage agents are sure a room is bugged, they can use a lightweight signal-strength meter to track it down. These handwheld devices require no tuning and show a stronger signal the closer they are to the source.

Spy-catching

LOCATING AND IDENTIFYING SPIES is rarely easy – unless a double agent or defector betrays them. Suspicious radio signals can sometimes allow counterintelligence agents to pinpoint a hidden transmitter. By tapping telephones and secretly opening mail, a counterspy can find a few spies, and patient surveillance catches many more. Careless spies sometimes give themselves away when collecting intelligence. For example, following a suspected spy can lead to the discovery of other unknown agents. Once they are caught, they must be "neutralized." This can mean exposing them so they cannot work secretly, expelling them to their home country, or prosecuting and imprisoning them. In some countries neutralization can have a more sinister meaning – a bogus trial and a death sentence.

Intelligence officers leave court carrying Bossard's spying equipment

BLEEPS TRACE MISSILE SECRET
A tip-off by a defector alerted Britain's MI5 to spy Frank Bossar (b.1912). They caught him by fixing a transmitter to the files h "borrowed" from his Air Ministr office. The transmitter's radio bleeps led MI5 officers to where t spy was copying the documents

Probe fits through slit at top of envelope and jaws grip the letter

SUSPICIOUS SPY-CATCHER
As counterespionage chief of the CIA, James Jesus Angleton (1917–87) hunted spies for two decades. He trusted nobody and suspected every defector of being a KGB double agent. He found few moles, however, and his intense suspicion slowed the agency's work. By ordering illegal mail interceptions, he damaged his reputation and was fired in 1974.

Winding handle rolls letter into tight coil

Applying invisible crayon sticks powders to a surface

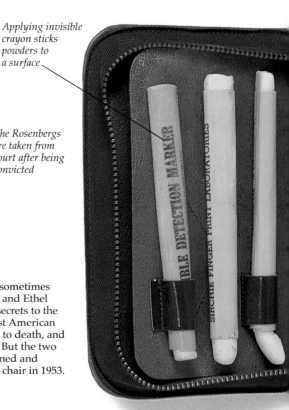

By pulling handle, agent pulls out letter

The Rosenbergs are taken from court after being convicted

FLAPS AND SEALS
Counterespionage agents use tools like this to open letters, read them, and replace them without tearing the envelope. This skill, known as "flaps and seals," allows them to monitor letters addressed to a spy. Letters mailed by the spy, however, are much more difficult to intercept.

ROUGH JUSTICE
Harsh punishment of spies has sometimes aroused strong emotions. Julius and Ethel Rosenberg were caught giving secrets to the Soviet Union. They were the first American peacetime spies to be sentenced to death, and many people begged for mercy. But the two Communist spies were condemned and were put to death in the electric chair in 1953.

SPIES ON VIDEO
Video surveillance can catch a spy at work, but checking tapes from many cameras is time-consuming. This may change with the development of digital cameras linked to computers. Once the software has "learned" what certain spies look like, it can pick them out in a crowd and start videotapes running to track the spy's movements.

...rveillance cameras ...be used to track a ...pect's movements

...MERSH agent's ...ntity card

Ultraviolet light reveals anti-bugging seals

SMERSH AGENCY
The Soviet counterespionage organization Smert Shpionam (roughly translated as "death to spies") was responsible for military security and for catching spies within the country's intelligence services. The agency soon acquired the nickname "SMERSH."

CHECKING SEALS
After a bugging sweep, counter-intelligence agents use seals to secure "clean" areas. An ultraviolet lamp is used to reveal the anti-bugging stickers to check they are not broken.

RED-HANDED
By dusting secret files with these special powders (left), counter-intelligence agents can catch a spy who handles the material. Powder sticking to the spy's hands glows under light from sources such as the ultraviolet lantern (above right).

Screen relays signals from satellite to track small craft off the Florida coast that may be carrying drugs

NEW WORK
Spy-catching no longer grabs headlines as it did in the Cold War, and former counterespionage officers now find they have other duties. The CIA, for example, has established a counter-narcotics center to coordinate the activities of the American intelligence organizations in the fight against drug trafficking.

Powder is invisible in normal light when sprinkled on files

Spying without spies

THE WORK OF REAL LIVE SPIES – or HUMINT (human intelligence) – is both costly and slow, and if a spy is discovered, it could embarrass politicians. Fortunately, there are some alternatives. Technical intelligence-gathering uses remote sensors that can do the spy's work from a distance. COMINT (communications intelligence); SIGINT (signals); ELINT (electronic); and IMINT (imagery) all provide valuable knowledge. Perhaps the most important is IMINT, which is the gathering of pictures from cameras and radar in spy aircraft and satellites. These provide amazing views of objects on the ground – some can even distinguish between civilians and soldiers. Just as satellites improve a spy's distant vision, technical intelligence below ground makes other senses keener. Seabed hydrophones track the sound of enemy submarines and, like sensitive fingertips, seismographs detect the vibrations caused by atomic tests.

SPY PLANES WITHOUT PILOTS
Darkstar is a drone, or unmanned aerial vehicle (UAV), developed in the United States. UAVs can take detailed air photographs of heavily defended enemy territory without risking a pilot's life.

SPY SATELLITE LAUNCH
Older spy satellites used film because the pictures produced were sharper than video. The film fell to Earth in a capsule for collection and processing. Such spy satellites are still secret. This Soviet launch carries a civilian version into orbit.

THE EARTH FROM SPACE
Multi-spectral images give intelligence agencies detailed pictures of war zones and military bases, but they do not show the landscape in true colors. In this image of Sarajevo in former Yugoslavia, electronic processing has made buildings stand out in pink. With greater enlargement, pictures can record objects as small as a truck.

Russian KFA satellite on ground after reentry

Engines power the Blackbird forward three times faster than the speed of sound

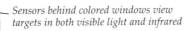
Sensors behind colored windows view targets in both visible light and infrared

EYES IN THE SKIES
American Keyhole 12 spy satellites can "see" objects as small as a grapefruit from a distance of 250 miles (400 km). No nation releases pictures of its spy satellites. However, this Earth observation satellite, which is used for map-making, is built in the same way. Radar imaging allows spy satellites to look straight through cloud cover, and infrared sensors can even pick out heat shadows left by a missile launch. Multi-spectral cameras in the satellite make it possible to distinguish between real trees and camouflage.

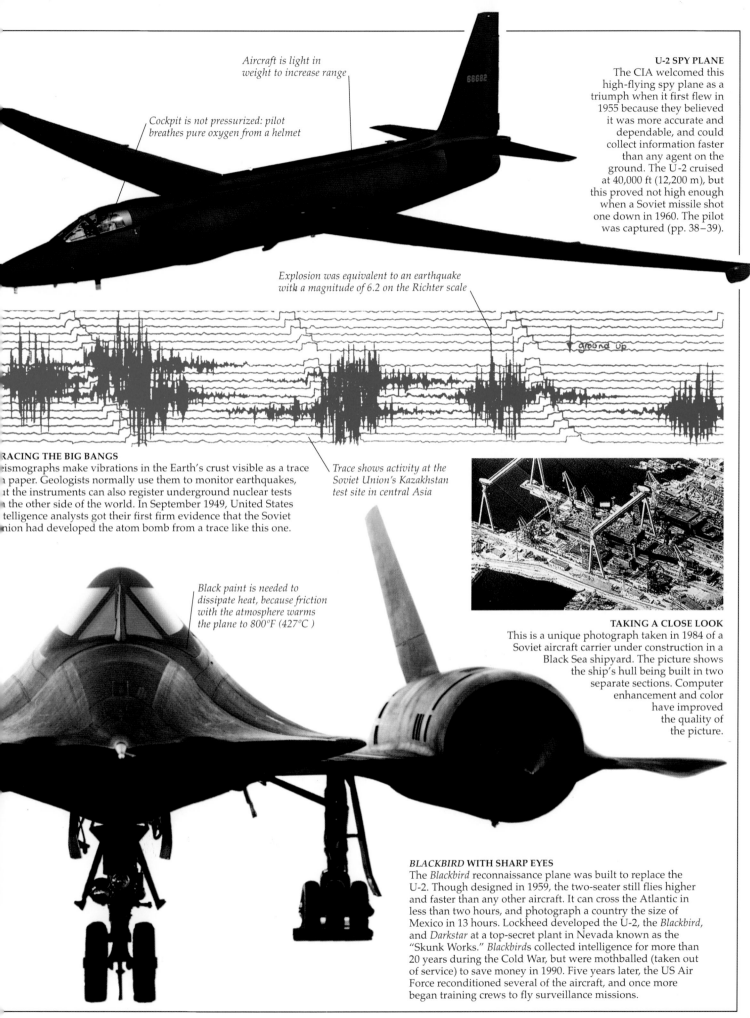

Aircraft is light in weight to increase range

Cockpit is not pressurized: pilot breathes pure oxygen from a helmet

66682

U-2 SPY PLANE

The CIA welcomed this high-flying spy plane as a triumph when it first flew in 1955 because they believed it was more accurate and dependable, and could collect information faster than any agent on the ground. The U-2 cruised at 40,000 ft (12,200 m), but this proved not high enough when a Soviet missile shot one down in 1960. The pilot was captured (pp. 38–39).

Explosion was equivalent to an earthquake with a magnitude of 6.2 on the Richter scale

ground up

TRACING THE BIG BANGS

Seismographs make vibrations in the Earth's crust visible as a trace on paper. Geologists normally use them to monitor earthquakes, but the instruments can also register underground nuclear tests on the other side of the world. In September 1949, United States intelligence analysts got their first firm evidence that the Soviet Union had developed the atom bomb from a trace like this one.

Trace shows activity at the Soviet Union's Kazakhstan test site in central Asia

Black paint is needed to dissipate heat, because friction with the atmosphere warms the plane to 800°F (427°C)

TAKING A CLOSE LOOK

This is a unique photograph taken in 1984 of a Soviet aircraft carrier under construction in a Black Sea shipyard. The picture shows the ship's hull being built in two separate sections. Computer enhancement and color have improved the quality of the picture.

BLACKBIRD WITH SHARP EYES

The *Blackbird* reconnaissance plane was built to replace the U-2. Though designed in 1959, the two-seater still flies higher and faster than any other aircraft. It can cross the Atlantic in less than two hours, and photograph a country the size of Mexico in 13 hours. Lockheed developed the U-2, the *Blackbird*, and *Darkstar* at a top-secret plant in Nevada known as the "Skunk Works." *Blackbird*s collected intelligence for more than 20 years during the Cold War, but were mothballed (taken out of service) to save money in 1990. Five years later, the US Air Force reconditioned several of the aircraft, and once more began training crews to fly surveillance missions.

Spying today

SPIES THRIVED DURING THE COLD WAR. While it lasted, the United States and the Soviet Union feared each other's bombs and missiles, and needed intelligence agencies to help keep the peace. When the Cold War ended in the late 1980s, many spies lost their jobs. Intelligence agencies had to adapt quickly. They looked for new uses for the spies' special skills and equipment, and some even formed alliances with scientists. For example, instead of tracking submarines, America's secret hydrophone network listened to the sound of whales. Spies found that their skills in counterespionage were just as useful in counterterrorism. Intelligence agents who had trailed Cold War traitors now followed Colombian drug barons. However, not all spies accepted the role of international law enforcer. In the chaos that followed the breakup of the Soviet Union, Russian farmers planted 100,000 fields with opium poppies. All they needed were people with the right international connections to distribute the heroin they made from the poppies. There was only one choice: they recruited some of Russia's newly out-of-work spies.

SKY-HIGH EYE
Satellite data helps environmentalists monitor climate change and loss of habitat because of human activity or natural disaster. Spy satellites take the sharpest pictures, but until recently these have been kept secret. Now the CIA is making its images available to the general public. They will give researchers a clearer picture of how earth has changed over the last 40 years.

DRUGS ON THE STREET
Intelligence agencies can collect information about the production and the smuggling of narcotics. However, the war on drugs does not end when shipments reach their destination. Kits like these (left) help agents catch drug dealers. The sprays quickly identify drugs wherever they are, avoiding the cost and delay of laboratory analysis.

EVER-CHANGING ROLE
However much the world changes, there will always be a role for secret agents. Russia may no longer threaten the United States, but war now endangers Eastern Europe, and CIA agents have learned to speak the local Serbo-Croatian language. U.S. Secret Service agents also have an important role to play in guarding the president.

DRUGS SNOOPER
The war against drugs increasingly relies on American satellites that were once used to police nuclear weapons treaties. High above Colombia, a "spy in the sky" can identify jungle landing strips, drug laboratories, and storage areas. Using information gathered by satellite pictures, Colombian soldiers swoop down on the bases with helicopters and ground troops. They seized 22 tons of cocaine in a single 1994 raid.

U.S. Secret Service man protects President Bush at an anti-drug summit

Shoulder bag conceals a machine gun

Fuel rod contains
pellets of nuclear
material

ighter-fluid
psules to add
flammability

FUELING FEAR
Terrorists need 15.5 lb (7 kg) of plutonium from a nuclear power
plant to build a bomb, and workers in Russia's crumbling nuclear
industry are happy to sell it. Intelligence services across the
world cooperate in tracing this stolen plutonium and uranium.

Plutonium sealed
inside is highly
poisonous, but
radiation it emits
is not a danger to
bomb-makers

Power source
(4 x 1.5-volt
batteries)

Timer
circuit
board

Timer
switch

Indicator
light

Power on/off switch

Compartment containing
incendiary device

Fire bomb was defused
before it could go off

A BOMB
1993 MI5 (Britain's counter-
pionage agency) joined the
olice in the hunt for the IRA (Irish
epublican Army) bombers. In the
st the IRA has used weapons such
this fire bomb in its campaign to
ite Northern Ireland (a British
ovince) with the Irish Republic.
I5 now uses its skills to track
wn other activists, including
me animal rights campaigners
ho also use fire bombs.

ORGANIZED CRIME
In the United States, the
FBI tracks spies and fights
organized crime gangs such
as the Mafia and the Chinese
Triads. Counterespionage
rganizations, such as MI5 in
Britain, have only recently
joined the police in the fight.

SHINING PATH
Behind bars, Abimael
Guzman no longer
leads the Shining Path
guerrilla movement that
terrorized Peru for more
than 20 years, killing
25,000 people. Police
used spy tactics to
catch him in 1992, first
collecting intelligence
and then staking out
his apartment with
agents in disguise.

Gamblers gather at the
headquarters of New
York's Hung Mon
Association, which
has direct links
with Triad gangs

Famous spies

THE MOST SUCCESSFUL SPIES do not become famous. As soon as their work is complete, they disappear into the shadows. Wartime spies are the exception to this. When the fighting ends, they tell their stories and sometimes earn high honors. As a reward for her spying, and for undergoing torture and imprisonment, Odette Sansom received one of Britain's most important medals, the George Cross. Not everybody believed that she deserved it. Yvonne Cormeau (pp. 32–33) complained that other SOE agents got lesser awards because "we haven't been caught." Of course all spies try to avoid capture, but if it happens, fame can quickly follow. Their captors are eager to put the spies' crimes on show. Spy trials often disappoint newspaper readers who follow them – in a real spy's life glamor is rare, and the routine boring. However, a few spies do live lives as exciting as any novel. Some actually turn into fictional characters: Ian Fleming based James Bond on the spy Dusko Popov.

Sean Connery as Bond in the film *Dr No*

WILL THE REAL SPY STAND UP?
Fictional James Bond (top) and real spy Dusko Popov (above with his wife) both enjoye gambling and the company of beautiful wome Bond's creator, Ian Fleming (pp. 58–59), met Popov in 1941 when they were both secret agen

For her stage act, Mata Hari wore elaborate costumes and headdresses, but often danced naked as well

Mata Hari falsely claimed that she was the daughter of a temple dancer and that she had been dedicated to the god Shiva

FAILED SPY
As Mata Hari, exotic dancer Margaretha Macleod (1876–1917) entertained German officers in France during World War I. Although she became one of the most famous names in the history of espionage, she was not very good at spying. She was recruited by the German Secret Service, but they did not entirely trust her, and she offered her services to the Allies. Germany finally betrayed her to France and on October 15, 1917, she was executed by a French firing squad.

CODE NAME "WHITE RABBIT"
Welsh Royal Air Force officer "Tommy" Yeo-Thomas became famous after his arrest and torture by the Gestapo, the German secret police, during World War II. He had been working for the SOE (pp. 32–33), organizing the French resistance to German troops occupying France. He was betrayed and captured outside a metro station in Paris. Tortured by the Gestapo, he was imprisoned but escaped from the death camp at Buchenwald in Germany.

Forged papers gave "White Rabbit" cover stories on his visits to France

nald Maclean (1913–83)
sed atom bomb
rets to Moscow

y Burgess (1911–63)
acted attention with
drunken violence

n Philby (1912–88)
rned Maclean and
rgess when to flee

thony Blunt (1907–83)
ped the others escape
he Soviet Union

Odette Sansom was the first woman to win the George Cross

Odette Samson
with the dolls
in 1954

Dolls entirely hand-sewn

Ski sticks made from card and silver foil

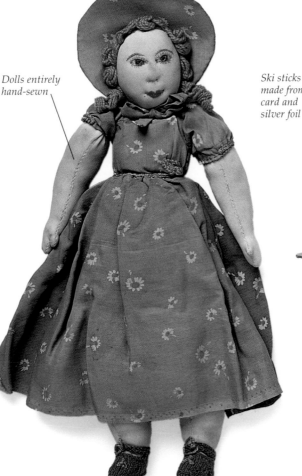

WARTIME HEROINE

During World War II, Odette Sansom (1931–95) worked as "Céline," an agent for the Allied Special Operations Executive (SOE). She helped organize resistance groups in southern France. Betrayed by a double agent in 1943, Odette was captured and taken to Fresnes Prison near Paris, where she was horribly tortured. After Fresnes, she was transferred to a prison in Germany and then to a concentration camp. Making these dolls for the nephew and niece of a German Catholic priest helped her pass the long hours of captivity. She was finally freed by the Allies in May 1945. The cruelty of her ordeal and the valor with which she faced it made her a legendary wartime spy.

THE CAMBRIDGE FIVE

Four of this century's most notorious spies met at Cambridge University, England. While working for Britain's Foreign Office, Guy Burgess and Donald Maclean leaked secrets to Moscow, fleeing there in 1951 when MI5 began to suspect them. When the "third man," Kim Philby (pp. 34–35), joined them in 1961, a "fourth man", Anthony Blunt, secretly admitted to spying. In return for his confession, Blunt kept his job as Surveyor of the Queen's Pictures until he retired. However, by 1979, his name had become public knowledge and, later, a "fifth man," John Cairncross, was revealed.

SHOW-TRIAL VICTIM

Soviet military intelligence officer Oleg Penkowsky (1919–63) contacted Western intelligence agencies in 1960. He believed he could prevent war by telling the West about Soviet nuclear missiles. The secrets he provided gave the United States a real advantage in the Cold War. The KGB caught Penkowsky and he was given a show trial at which he "confessed." He was sentenced to death and reportedly executed in 1963.

Spies in fiction

Michael Caine played Harry Palmer in the 1965 film version of The Ipcress File

ESPIONAGE HAS ALL THE INGREDIENTS for an exciting storybook or movie: suspense, action, intrigue, and natural drama. American author James Fenimore Cooper (1789–1851) helped establish the spy story with his book *The Spy* in 1851, but spy novels have only really become popular in the last 50 years. Some of the most successful authors were themselves spies. Ian Fleming worked for British naval intelligence during World War II. John Le Carré drew on his experience of MI5 and MI6 to create a more authentic picture of the secret agent's world. Hollywood turned the books of both authors and many more into successful movies, but the books and films did not always impress real spies. Allen Dulles, once head of the CIA, wrote that "spy heroes...rarely exist in real life." This did not stop the CIA from using spy films to train agents on the finer points and pitfalls of their trade.

ANTI-HERO
In *The Ipcress File*, writer Len Deighton created a spy hero who shared only his nationality with James Bond. The story of the Cockney-petty-criminal-turned-reluctant-spy was Deighton's hugely successful first book.

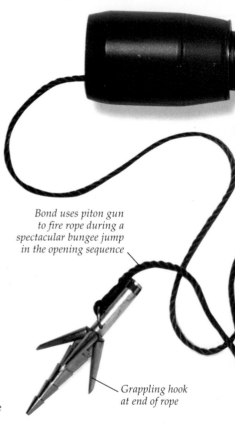

Bond uses piton gun to fire rope during a spectacular bungee jump in the opening sequence

Grappling hook at end of rope

AUTHOR MEETS SPY
Frederick Forsyth (left) based his book *The Odessa File* on the exploits of the German "Champagne Spy" Wolfgang Lotz (right). Lotz crippled the Egyptian missile program, helping Israel win the Six-Day War against Egypt in 1967.

Lotz's high lifestyle earned him his nickname of "the Champagne Spy"

SPY HIT LIST
British spies may not be the world's best, but the country's espionage writers top the bestseller lists. In the 1960s, their anti-Communist message alarmed the KGB. The Soviets hit back with *The Zakhov Mission*, in which a Communist hero defeats 007. It could not compete with the success of Fleming's originals, which have been translated all over the world.

FICTIONAL EVIL LADY
"We are enveloped in a network of spies," cries D'Artagnan, the young hero who helps the Three Musketeers in the famous adventure story written by Alexandre Dumas (1802–1870). Milady (right) is the most deadly of the spies who are employed by Cardinal Richelieu (pp. 40–41) to try and discredit the queen of France.

INDIAN ROPE TRICK
High-tech gadgetry is as much the star in a Bond film as 007 himself. In the Bond books, Ian Fleming based these devices on genuine inventions supplied by people such as Charles Fraser-Smith to World War II agents (pp. 12–13).

Buckle conceals 75-ft (27-m) long fine rope that can bear Bond's weight

Bond's belt worn in the film Goldeneye

Telescopic sights

TIME TOOL
Watches play a leading role in many of the Bond films. In *Goldeneye*, a laser built into Bond's watch helps him cut his way out of difficult situations. The KGB studied James Bond films in order to develop their own spy technology.

James Bond's piton gun from the film *Goldeneye*

Piton gun contains laser which Bond uses to cut open the roof of a Russian chemical plant

LICENSED TO PRINT MONEY
When Ian Fleming (1908–64) created the character of James Bond, he was aiming to write the spy story "to end all spy stories." His 12 Bond books sold more than 18 million copies.

In Goldeneye, the seventeenth James Bond film, Pierce Brosnan plays the sophisticated British spy

Bond primes a magnetic mine to destroy the chemical plant

True-to-life bugging tool kit includes lock-pick gun

BUGGED BATHROOM
In the film *The Conversation*, a bugging expert (played by Gene Hackman) is drawn into a terrifying world of deception and murder. As nerve-wracking as any political spy story, the film is a rare and authentic glimpse of the work of industrial espionage agents.

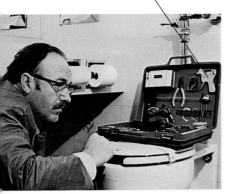

Index

Acknowledgments

Dorling Kindersley would like to thank:
Audiotel International Limited (Keith Penny, Ray Summers, Julie Walker, Adrian Hickey); Eon Productions (Julie O'Reilly); the Imperial War Museum, London (Paul Cornish, John Bullen, Mike Hibbard); Intelligence Corps Museum, Ashford (Major R.W.M. Shaw, Mrs. Janet Carpenter); Leica UK Ltd. (Peter Mulder); Lorraine Electronics Surveillance (David Benn, Simon Rosser); H. Keith Melton; Next Retail Ltd. (Shirley Brown, Hilary Santell); Joanne Poynor; Spycatcher (Mike Phillips); Whitbread plc. (Nicholas Redman, Archivist).

Design help: Ann Cannings, Jason Gonsalves, Sailesh Patel. Pigeon: Rick Osman. Pigeon parachute: Martine Cooper.

Artwork: John Woodcock

Endpapers: Iain Morris

Index: Marion Dent

Picture credits
The publisher would like to thank the following for their kind permission to reproduce the photographs:

(a = above, b = below, c = center, l = left, r = right, t = top)

AKG Photos, London: J.V. Leffdoel, Scipio Publius Cornelius 40tl.
Ancient Art & Architecture Collection: 8tl, 8bl, 8bc.
Associated Press Ltd.: 11tr, 29bl, 35t, 35br, 43c, 47bl, 52tr; Wire Photo 53cr.
Aviation Photographs International: 38tl.
Bildarchiv Preussischer Kulturbesitz: 25cl.
Bilderdienst Süddeutscher Verlag: 27cl.
Bridgeman Art Library, London/New York: Guildhall Art Gallery, Corporation of London, Sir John Gilbert, detail from Ego Et Rex Meus 40cl; Private Collection, I. Glasunov Ivan the Terrible, 1989, 40bl; by courtesy of the board of Trustees of the V & A, London, Nicholas Hilliard, Mary Queen of Scots 28cl.
Camera Press Ltd.: 35tr, 39cl; R. Artacho 55br; S. Ferguson 42br; B. Ross 56ra.

Jean-Loup Charmet: Bibliothèque des Arts Decoratifs, Lucien Laforge L'Espion, 1916, 31tc.
DC Comics, Inc.: Spy vs. Spy is a trademark of E.C. Publications, Inc. © 1995. All rights reserved. Used with permission 42t.
Eon Productions: Keith Hamshere/United Artists ('GOLDEN EYE') front cover bcl, 4cb, 9br, 59tr, 59cr, 59br, 58-59.
Mary Evans Picture Library: front flap tl, 29r, 40c; J. Mammen back cover tl, 14tl.
E.T. Archive: Biblioteca Nazionale Marciana, Venice 9tr; Musée Versailles, Philippe de Champaigne, detail from Cardinal Richelieu 41cr; Staatliche Glyptothek, Munich 9tl; V & A, London 11tc.
Werner Forman Archive: Ninja Museum Ueno, detail showing Ninja making secret signs 40bl; E. Strouhal 8bl.
Ronald Grant Archive: Stakeout 1987, Touchstone 16bl; Doctor No, 1962, UA/Eon 56tr; The Ipcress File 1965, Rank/Steven Lowndes 58tr; The Three Musketeers 1948, MGM 58br; The Conversation 1974, Paramount/Francis Ford Coppola 59bl.
Michael Holford: Musée de Bayeux 8-9; V & A, London 10-11.
Hulton Deutsch Collection: 10cr, 38c, 41c, 41bl, 56l, 57tc, 57br, 57l.
Imperial War Museum, London: 23bc, 29tl, 36tr, 56br; Fougasse, Careless Talk Costs Lives 10tr.
Lockheed: 52-53.
Lockheed Martin Skunk Works: 53t.
Magnum Photos Ltd.: E. Erwitt 43cl; S. Meiselas 54bl; E. Reed 19cr; A. Webb 51br; Zachmann 55bl.
The Mansell Collection: 10tl.
H. Keith Melton: front cover br and bcr, back cover rcb, 12br, 13tl, 13tc, 13bl, 23cl, 27cr, 28tl, 28cr, 28tr, 28br, 30br, 36br, 37tl, 37tr, 37c, 37b, 42bl, 43tl, 43tr, 43br, 45tl, 50l, 50-51lb, 51cl; Jerry Richards of the FBI Laboratory, Washington D.C. 10cl, 10c; Jack Ingram, Curator of the National Cryptologic Museum, Maryland 16cl, 16c, 27tr.
Mirror Syndication International: 27b, 50tr; Aldus Archive 24tl; Aldus Archive/Science Museum/Eileen

Tweedy front cover cr, 24cl; Rijksinstituut voor Oorlogsdocumentatie 9c; National Archives, USA 26c; Public Record Office 25tl, 41tl; © US Army 27tl.
National Cryptologic Museum, Maryland: 26bl.
National Portrait Gallery, London: John De Critz, the Elder Sir Francis Walsingham 41tr.
Peter Newark's American Pictures: 30tl, 30bc, 31bl.
Popperfoto: 23tl, 31tr, 31br, 35bl, 41br, 58cl; Reuter/S. Jaffe 34br; Reuter/W. McNamee 34c.
Press Association: 36bcl.
Range: Bettmann/UPI 22bl, 50c, 54br; Bettmann/UPI/Sam Schulman 50bc.
Rex Features Ltd.: Action Press 38-39; Sipa-Press 39tl.
Reuters Television: front cover tl, 42cr (detail), 54tl (detail).
Science Photo Library: NRSC Ltd. 52c; R. Ressmeyer, Starlight 38bc.
Science & Society Picture Library, Science Museum, London: 26tl.
Frank Spooner Pictures: Gamma-Liaison 11cl.
Topham-Picturepoint Ltd.: back cover br, 12tl, 35cla, 35c, 34tl, 34tr; AP 45tc.
Worldmap-Priroda: 52tl, 52bl.

SUBJECTS

HISTORY

AFRICA

ANCIENT CHINA

ARMS & ARMOR

BATTLE

CASTLE

COWBOY

EXPLORER

KNIGHT

MEDIEVAL LIFE

MYTHOLOGY

NORTH AMERICAN INDIAN

PIRATE

PRESIDENTS

RUSSIA

SHIPWRECK

TITANIC

VIKING

WITCHES & MAGIC-MAKERS

ANCIENT WORLDS

ANCIENT EGYPT

ANCIENT GREECE

ANCIENT ROME

AZTEC, INCA & MAYA

BIBLE LANDS

MUMMY

PYRAMID

THE BEGINNINGS OF LIFE

ARCHEOLOGY

DINOSAUR

EARLY HUMANS

PREHISTORIC LIFE

THE ARTS

BOOK

COSTUME

DANCE

FILM

MUSIC

TECHNOLOGY

BOAT

CAR

FLYING MACHINE

FUTURE

INVENTION

SPACE EXPLORATION

TRAIN

PAINTING

GOYA

IMPRESSIONISM

LEONARDO & HIS TIMES

MANET

MONET

PERSPECTIVE

RENAISSANCE

VAN GOGH

WATERCOLOR

SCIENCE

ASTRONOMY

CHEMISTRY

EARTH

ECOLOGY

ELECTRICITY

ELECTRONICS

ENERGY

EVOLUTION

FORCE & MOTION

HUMAN BODY

LIFE

LIGHT

MATTER

MEDICINE

SKELETON

TECHNOLOGY

TIME & SPACE

SPORT

BASEBALL

FOOTBALL

OLYMPICS

SOCCER

SPORTS

ANIMALS

AMPHIBIAN

BIRD

BUTTERFLY & MOTH

CAT

DOG

EAGLE &
BIRDS OF PREY

ELEPHANT

FISH

GORILLA,
MONKEY & APE

HORSE

INSECT

MAMMAL

REPTILE

SHARK

WHALE

HABITATS

ARCTIC & ANTARCTIC

DESERT

JUNGLE

OCEAN

POND & RIVER

SEASHORE

THE EARTH

CRYSTAL & GEM

FOSSIL

HURRICANE &
TORNADO

PLANT

ROCKS & MINERALS

SHELL

TREE

VOLCANO &
EARTHQUAKE

WEATHER

THE WORLD
AROUND US

BUILDING

CRIME & DETECTION

FARM

FLAG

MEDIA &
COMMUNICATIONS

MONEY

RELIGION

SPY

Future updates and editions will be available online at www.dk.com

DK EYEWITNESS BOOKS

A–Z

DK EYEWITNESS BOOKS

1–110

Future updates and editions will be available online at www.dk.com